VAUGHAN PUBLIC LIBRARIES
3 3288 08558514 1

D1224282

THE HUMAN POPULATION

GLOBAL CONNECTIONS

America's Role in a Changing World
Changing Climates
The Changing Global Economy
Environment and Natural Resources
Feeding a Hungry World
The Human Population
Human Rights
One World or Many?
Pandemics and Global Health
Terrorism and Security

THE HUMAN POPULATION

CHARLES F. GRITZNER

This book is affectionately dedicated to Catherine M. Lockwood, who opened my eyes to viewing the human population "problem" as a cutural, rather than a demographic, issue.

The Human Population

Chelsea House
An imprint of Infobase Publishing
132 West 31st Street
New York, NY 10001

Library of Congress Cataloging-in-Publication Data
Gritzner, Charles F.
The human population / by Charles F. Gritzner.
p. cm. — (Global connections)
Includes bibliographical references and index.
ISBN 978-1-60413-288-5 (hardcover)
1. Population. 2. Population forecasting. I. Title. II. Series.

HB871.G85 2009
363.9—dc22 2008054880

Chelsea House books are available at special discounts when purchased in bulk quantities for businesses, associations, institutions, or sales promotions. Please call our Special Sales Department in New York at (212) 967-8800 or (800) 322-8755.

You can find Chelsea House on the World Wide Web at http://www.chelseahouse.com

Text design and composition by Annie O'Donnell
Cover design by Takeshi Takahashi
Cover printed by IBT Global, Inc., Troy, NY
Book printed and bound by IBT Global, Inc., Troy, NY
Date printed: March 2011
Printed in the United States of America

10 9 8 7 6 5 4 3 2

This book is printed on acid-free paper.

All links and Web addresses were checked and verified to be correct at the time of publication. Because of the dynamic nature of the Web, some addresses and links may have changed since publication and may no longer be valid.

CONTENTS

INTRODUCTION

A GLOBAL COMMUNITY

Globalization is the process of coming together as a closely connected global community. It began thousands of years ago, when tribal groups and small hunting parties wandered from place to place. The process accelerated following Columbus's epic voyage more than five centuries ago. Europeans—an estimated 50 million of them—spread out to occupy lands throughout the world. This migration transformed the distribution of the world's peoples and their cultures forever. In the United States and Canada, for example, most people speak a West European language. Most practice a religious faith with roots in the ancient Middle East and eat foods originating in Asia.

Today, we are citizens of a closely interwoven global community. Events occurring half a world away can be watched and experienced, often as they happen, in our own homes. People, materials, and even diseases can be transported from continent to continent in a single day, thanks to jet planes. Electronic communications make possible the instantaneous exchange of information by phone, e-mail, or other means with friends or business associates almost anywhere in the world. Trade and commerce, perhaps more so than any other aspect of our daily lives, amply illustrate the importance of global linkages. How many things in your home (including your clothing) are of international origin? What foods and beverages have you consumed today that came from other lands? Could Northern America's economy survive without foreign oil, iron ore, copper, or other vital resources?

The GLOBAL CONNECTIONS series is designed to help you realize how closely people and places are tied to one another within the expanding global community. Each book introduces you to political, economic, environmental, social, medical, and other timely issues, problems, and prospects. The authors and editors hope you enjoy and learn from these books. May they hand you a passport to intellectual travels throughout our fascinating, complex, and increasingly "intradependent" world!

—Charles F. Gritzner
Consulting Editor

INTRODUCTION TO POPULATION

In early 2009, the human population reached 6,750,000,000, about 306,000,000 of whom were Americans. During the previous year, the world's population grew by about 77 million. That is about a quarter of the U.S. population and more than double Canada's 33 million people. Worldwide, the population is growing by about 1.2 percent each year. If current trends continue, most estimates place human numbers at around 9 to 9.5 billion by 2050. Life expectancy in the United States and Canada is about 79 years. When most readers of this book reach retirement age, there will be 30 percent more people than are now living!

Are these figures cause for alarm? Will there be enough food for everyone? Will there be adequate space for another nearly 3 billion people? What about supplies of fuel, water, metals, and other important natural resources? Will there be a struggle for survival that will further split the world into have and have-not populations? Is the world suffering from a terrible population "explosion"? These are just some of the difficult questions that this book will attempt to answer.

How you answered the foregoing questions can say a great deal about you. Readers from the United States or Canada, which rank among the world's most highly developed lands, will answer much differently than readers living in the world's poorest nations. Many factors influence the way we think about population. A person's political and religious beliefs, for example, can strongly influence views on such issues as migration and family planning. Ethnicity (cultural heritage) and race (biological inheritance) can affect the way one thinks about population growth and immigration. The type of work or business in which an individual is involved can also influence attitudes toward various aspects of population. Today, in many countries around the globe, few issues are more controversial or debates more heated than those relating to population.

It seems that most everyone has an "answer" to the population "problem." Unfortunately, the answers are often naïve and simplistic. This author has taught population geography for more than three decades. One question I frequently ask students is whether the world is "overpopulated." Students are asked to provide some support for their answer. As often as not, the response is "Yes!" Their explanations, however, raise as many questions as they solve. Examples include: "There are too many people," "There is not enough food for everyone," or "There is too little space resulting in too much crowding."

As you will soon realize, population is one of the most important, yet one of the most complex, issues facing humankind today. To illustrate this point, let us return to the student responses from the previous paragraph. It may surprise you to know that "overpopulation" actually has little, if anything, to do with numbers of people. As you will learn, the condition results from a combination of factors. As for a link between population and poverty, some of the world's most densely populated countries also enjoy the world's highest standards of living.

Images such as this one, taken in a crowded train station in Mumbai, India, make it easy to believe that the world is quickly becoming overpopulated. The truth, however, might surprise you.

Many countries with very low population densities, on the other hand, are extremely poor. In regard to food, there is plenty to go around. The problem is one of distribution, not availability. As for space, 90 percent of the world's people live on less than 10 percent of the land area. There is plenty of space for everyone.

POPULATION AS A GLOBAL ISSUE

Population affects all of us in many ways. In some ways its impact is direct, such as trying to drive on a crowded freeway in rush hour traffic. In other ways, it is indirect. High prices at the gas pump, for example, may influence a family's decision of whether to take a vacation. One reason fuel costs are so high is

A GLOBAL COMMUNITY OF 1,000 PEOPLE

Based upon current figures, if the human population were a global community of 1,000 people, it would look something like this:

Where do they live?

820 live in economically less developed countries (LDCs)
180 live in economically developed lands
500 live in cities and 500 live in rural areas
610 are Asians (200 of whom are Chinese and 170 are from India)
140 are Africans
110 live in Europe (including Russia)
80 live in North America (about 46 of whom live in the United States and 4 in Canada)
60 are South Americans (30 of them in Brazil)
3 live in Australia

Who are they?

503 are men and 497 are women

that many of China's 1.3 billion people now own automobiles, a recent development. Their country's rapidly growing thirst for fuel has helped drive up gas prices because there is not enough supply to meet demand. In Northern America (the United States and Canada), about 30 percent of the corn crop is used to make ethanol. When corn is used as fuel for vehicles, less of it is available to feed people and livestock. This, in turn, drives up the cost of grain in distant and often much poorer lands.

People must consume food and beverages and use various raw materials and natural resources. Our very survival depends upon both. Yet, today, little relationship exists between where people live and where large amounts of food are produced. The same holds true for the connection between distribution of

280 are under 15 years of age and only 70 are 65 or older
9 will die during the coming year
21 babies will be born during the coming year
20 will be born to parents living in poor countries
9 suffer from HIV/AIDS
790 can read
330 are Christian (210 are Muslims and 160 claim no religious faith)

What do they have?

10 people control 40 percent of the world's wealth
100 people own 85 percent of the world's assets
500 people share only 1 percent of global wealth
500 own cell phones
14 have computers
12 have a college degree

human settlement and location of various natural resources. It is the global connections of trade and commerce that link people with essential foodstuffs and resources. Unfortunately, wealth is not evenly distributed globally. People in some regions of the world are able to buy food, raw materials, and natural resources. They are able to enjoy comfortable lives. Perhaps two-thirds of the world's population, however, lives in relative poverty. In poor lands, many people struggle to meet their day-to-day needs.

What does this geographical separation of people and what they need to survive mean in global terms? How, for example, can distant Africans or Asians have any influence whatsoever on a farmer living on the Interior Plains of Northern America? A farmer in South Dakota, a state that is heavily dependent upon agriculture, may wonder, "Why should we spend tax money to teach our youngsters about distant lands and people? Foreigners aren't important to us!" In fact, they are very important. The price the farmer receives for his crops, for example, is largely dependent upon foreign crop yields and markets. He also raises livestock for market. In today's economy, the sale of crops and livestock is not limited to a local market. Through the process of globalization, the "neighborhood" market now extends worldwide.

China is home to 1.3 billion people and India is home to 1.2 billion. Both countries are experiencing vigorous economic growth. When income increases, people spend more money on food. How will this affect the global flow, and therefore the availability and cost, of such commodities as grain, fruit, vegetables, and meat? How might the rapidly improving standard of living of several billion Asians directly affect the South Dakota farmer's income? How might *you* be affected?

Many countries face what some people believe to be an immigration crisis. In the United States, undocumented immigration has become a very hot political, economic, and social issue. (Although perhaps less controversial, migration has changed the ethnicity of Canada's population even more than that of the

Why do people in some areas of the world have an abundance of food while others don't have enough? Population has less of an impact on world hunger than do economics and government. Although food is easily distributed around the globe, poverty and corruption can mean that some people go hungry.

United States during recent decades.) Today, many towns and cities, and even large areas of the country, are being dramatically changed by immigration. Views are sharply divided in regard to the benefits or drawbacks of so many new immigrants. So are ideas on what to do about the "immigration problem." These are just some of the ways in which population issues, whether directly or indirectly, affect us all.

WHY DEMOGRAPHY IS IMPORTANT

Demography is the scientific study of the human population. Demographers use statistics and other data to explain the composition (makeup) of various populations. They also look at the distribution and density of people and try to understand and explain differences in these patterns. Finally, they attempt to understand and explain various changes and trends within the human population.

The links between demography and geography are very close. As geographer Glenn Trewartha once suggested, "Population serves as the point of reference from which all other [human] elements are observed, and from which they all, singly and collectively, derive significance and meaning." This certainly is true in regard to the social studies. Throughout this book, two soundly geographic ways of viewing the world will be used repeatedly. It is hoped that they will help the reader understand the importance of population.

First, geographers have their own way of studying differences that exist from place to place on Earth's surface. Basically, they ask, "What is where, why is it there, and why should we care?" The "what" can be any feature or condition—either physical or human—that exists. In this book, the "what" is anything and everything relating to the human population. "Where," obviously, refers to the location and distribution of various population-related conditions. Once scientists know where things are, the next step in problem solving can be taken. They try to explain the distribution by asking why this particular feature or condition is located in this particular place. Finally, they ask, "Why is this important to us?" These are questions to which we will return time and time again throughout this book.

The second geographic approach is to search for relationships between and among features and conditions. Once these relationships are identified, conditions are much easier to explain. A very close relationship exists in many regions, for example, between low population density and physical conditions such as severe cold or aridity. The tie between these two can be seen clearly by comparing maps of population distribution and world climates. High birth rates tend to occur in rural areas and regions of poverty. Cities, on the other hand, tend to have very low birth rates. Today most migration is from areas of relative poverty to regions in the economically developed world. Maps of migration and economic data clearly show this relationship. Throughout the book, please keep these two approaches in mind. Constantly ask yourself why certain conditions are found in particular locations. When a particular condition occurs, try to explain it to yourself. You will want to begin by looking for one or more other factors that influence it.

POPULATION DATA

Were one to believe the numbers presented by the U.S. Census Bureau Population Clock, the human population is known precisely and to the minute! To find the current U.S. and world population, you may simply go to the following Web site: http://www.census.gov/main/www/popclock.html.

HOW ACCURATE ARE POPULATION FIGURES?

How correct do you believe the population clock numbers (or, for that matter, any other population figures) really are? The answer "not very!" might surprise you. Actually, few if any population figures that appear in textbooks, the news media, or even "official" sources are precise. Why is this true? There are many reasons.

Some countries take a detailed census on a regular basis, usually every 10 years, but many do not. The frequency of census taking, the information gathered, and the accuracy of data vary greatly from country to country. Published population figures can be widely off the mark, even those for developed countries. For less developed countries (LDCs), population information is often little more than guesswork. All demographic information must be viewed with some caution.

At the time of the 2000 U.S. census, about $6 billion was spent on the head count that employed some 860,000 workers. Yet it is estimated that the enumerators (people who conducted the census) missed counting an estimated 6.5 million people. That is about 2 percent of the country's population! Further, the number of undocumented foreigners now in the United States is estimated at 12 million. How many of them have been counted? Twelve million people would represent 4 percent of the total U.S. population. If the United States can not accurately count its people, how can countries with fewer resources be expected to do an adequate job?

Can you imagine the difficulty of counting heads in a country such as China (1.3 billion) or India (1.2 billion)? Sheer numbers alone make the task all but impossible. Roughly two-thirds of the people in those countries are rural. This makes the task of finding and counting them even more difficult. Even developed countries often lag behind. Germany, for example, has not taken a census since reunification brought together East Germany and West Germany in 1990, and its next official count is not scheduled until 2011. Over a period of more than two decades, populations can change greatly.

There are many other problems associated with census taking. Despite the importance of census information, many people are leery of the process. Some are simply afraid to be found by census takers. Others are afraid to tell the truth. Why the fear? The origin of the word *census* provides a clue: It comes from the Latin word *censere,* meaning "to tax" or "to value." The sole purpose of many early censuses was to determine a country's tax base. In some lands, a census was conducted to find out how many young men were available for military service. Even today, in many countries

Census enumerators take thumbprints on home visits in Lagos, Nigeria, on March 22, 2006. Gathering population data is a challenge, particularly in developing nations.

(such as Nigeria, which is divided between Christians and Muslims) some people hesitate to be counted because of their religion. They fear that revealing their faith may expose them to bullying (or worse). For these and other reasons, in some countries it has been—and continues to be—in an individual's best interest to lie, or *not* to be counted. The following list spotlights some of the problems associated with census taking.

1. **When people are counted.** Gathering census information takes a great deal of time. In some countries, the process can last for months. Yet, over time, numbers change. For this reason, many countries establish what is called a "census moment." In the United States, it is midnight on April 1 of each year ending in "0." No

matter the span of time over which data are collected, all information is based upon that moment. Canada conducts a census every five years, the next being scheduled for May 10, 2011.

2. **Where people are counted.** Some countries count people where they are at the census moment. With so many people constantly moving about, this method can give a very inaccurate picture of where people actually live. Other countries, including the United States, count people at their normal place of residence regardless of their location at the census moment. This policy creates yet another issue: taxation. Should people be counted where they sleep or where they work? Today, many people earn their income in one place and live in another. Yet their taxes are usually paid where they live, rather than in the community where they work. This is a major reason why so many large American cities are run down and struggle to provide adequate services.
3. **Locating everyone.** In an increasingly mobile world, locating people can pose a huge problem. Additionally, census takers may face problems attempting to enter urban slums, isolated rural areas, or areas settled by hostile ethnic groups.
4. **Cost.** Taking a census is very costly. Many countries simply cannot afford the expense. It is estimated that the 2010 U.S. census will cost $11.3 billion, or about $37 to count each *individual*! The results, however, will determine not only congressional representation. They will also determine how some $200 billion in government funds will be distributed annually among states and other demographic units.
5. **Determining age.** Determining age also poses problems in some countries. In many parts of Asia, for example, the age count begins at birth. A person who has lived for one year is "two" on his or her first

birthday. Throughout the less developed world, many people have no idea of their age. Birth records may not be kept. In fact, many people (particularly the elderly) are unable to count. In terms of global record keeping, there is still another problem. Not all calendars (hence "years") are 365¼ days long!

6. **"White lies."** In many cultures, people may tell "white lies" to boast or to hide the truth from outsiders. What they try to hide, of course, varies from culture to cul-

VISUALIZING THE WORLD'S POPULATION

There are different ways of looking at the world's population. It is easy to develop a scenario that will support one's personal view of the population "controversy." As you read the following, decide whether the figures are those preferred by people who believe we are in a population crisis or those who believe that population numbers alone are not the real issue.

- If the world's population was lined up head to toe between Earth and the Moon (average height of 5 feet, or 1.5 meters, and a distance of 250,000 miles, or 400,000 kilometers), there would be nearly 25 human chains linking Earth and the Moon. New chains would grow about 80,000 miles (129,000 km) each year.
- An estimated 6 to 10 percent of all people who ever lived are living today.
- If dropped into Arizona's Grand Canyon, the human population would be nearly out of sight, filling only about one-tenth of the canyon's space.
- If the human population was placed head to toe around Earth's equator (ca. 25,000 miles; 40,200 km)—assuming an

ture. Even in the United States, many people are not truthful when giving information to census takers. Women, for example, may not give their actual age. Men, on the other hand, often lie about their income. Both men and women often "inflate" some figures. This is particularly common in regard to schooling and annual income. Many people hesitate to reveal whether they are divorced, living together but unmarried, or in a gay or lesbian union.

average height of 5 feet (1.5 m) per person—one continuous chain would contain about 26,400,000 people, and the total population would encircle the planet about 250 times. At the present rate of population increase, more than three new lines would be added each year.

- If each person on Earth was standing erect and occupying a space of three square feet (1 sq m), the population would cover approximately 630 square miles (1,632 sq km), or an area roughly 20 miles by 30 miles (32 km by 48 km).
- If each of the world's people occupied two feet of space in a standing line, as at a movie theater, the line would be 2,462,000 miles (3,962,000 km) long. It would circle Earth at the equator about 98.5 times. The line would grow at a rate of about 85 miles (137 km) each day, or about 1.2 times around Earth at the equator each year.
- If all the world's families had a home and one-eighth acre (.05 hectare) of farmland (the average size of a family's farm plot in Asia), all people on Earth and their small farms would occupy an area approximately the size of Texas or Canada's Alberta Province.

7. **Race or ethnicity.** Many censuses seek information on race and ethnicity. In some countries, including the United States and Canada, this can pose a problem. Worldwide, both biological (racial) and ethnic (cultural) mixing are widespread. Today, a rapidly growing percentage of the world's people are of mixed ancestry. They simply do not know or, for that matter, care what their racial or ethnic background is.

CENSUS DATA

A census is the single most important source of statistical information about a country or other defined political unit, such as a state, province, or municipality. Counts of people have been conducted for a very long time. So have censuses of property, agricultural production, buildings, and other features. The Bible's Old Testament contains several references to censuses as early as the fifteenth century B.C. By 550 B.C., a census had been taken of the citizens and property in the vicinity of Rome. In A.D. 1086, William the Conqueror conducted a famous and very detailed survey of landholders and holdings in Great Britain. The information has been used by geographers and historians to reconstruct life and settlement in Britain nearly 1,000 years ago.

The information collected during a census varies from country to country and even census to census. Several decades ago, the United Nations (UN) attempted to standardize the data collected. The international organization recommended that all censuses obtain the following information: total population; sex; age; marital status; place of birth; citizenship (country of official residence); nationality (how one answers the question "what are you?); mother's language; educational level and literacy; economic status; rural or urban place of residence; relationship of household members; and fertility rates (the number of children born to a woman during her childbearing years). Not all countries, including the United States and Canada, comply with all of the UN recommendations.

THE U.S. CENSUS

The U.S. census was the very first to be required by a country's constitution and taken on a regular interval. As a result, the country has conducted a census each decade, in every year ending in "0," since 1790.

The country's founding fathers established a Congress with two houses: a Senate and a House of Representatives. Each state sends two members to the Senate. The number of members a state elects to the House of Representatives, however, is determined by its population. In other words, a state's population determines the number of people who represent it in the House. Every decade, the census count is used to determine (re)apportionment—the number of representatives each state is eligible to send to Congress. The House of Representatives has 435 members, a number that does not change from election to election. As state populations change, the number of representatives from a state can change. For example, following the 2000 census, eight states gained one or more representatives. Eleven others, however, lost one or more House seats.

Early U.S. censuses were often quite detailed. Everyone was asked more than two dozen questions. In 2000, the number was reduced to eight on the short questionnaire. (A small number of people received a much longer and more detailed census form.) The information gathered from everyone included: name, address, household relationship, sex, race, age, marital status, and whether of Hispanic/Latino/Spanish origin or descent.

WHY IS CENSUS INFORMATION IMPORTANT?

Census information is essential for many reasons other than congressional apportionment. It gives a profile of population makeup for a specified area. For example, a census may compile information on place of residence, sex, age, number of children, and marital status. This information can be used to determine

United States **Census 2000**

U.S. Department of Commerce • Bureau of the Census

This is the official form for all the people at this address. It is quick and easy, and your answers are protected by law. Complete the Census and help your community get what it needs — today and in the future!

Start Here **Please use a black or blue pen.**

1. How many people were living or staying in this house, apartment, or mobile home on April 1, 2000?

Number of people

INCLUDE in this number:
- foster children, roomers, or housemates
- people staying here on April 1, 2000 who have no other permanent place to stay
- people living here most of the time while working, even if they have another place to live

DO NOT INCLUDE in this number:
- college students living away while attending college
- people in a correctional facility, nursing home, or mental hospital on April 1, 2000
- Armed Forces personnel living somewhere else
- people who live or stay at another place most of the time

2. Is this house, apartment, or mobile home — *Mark* ☒ *ONE box.*
- ☐ Owned by you or someone in this household with a mortgage or loan?
- ☐ Owned by you or someone in this household free and clear (without a mortgage or loan)?
- ☐ Rented for cash rent?
- ☐ Occupied without payment of cash rent?

3. Please answer the following questions for each person living in this house, apartment, or mobile home. Start with the name of one of the people living here who owns, is buying, or rents this house, apartment, or mobile home. If there is no such person, start with any adult living or staying here. We will refer to this person as Person 1.

What is this person's name? *Print name below.*

Last Name

First Name MI

OMB No. 0607-0856: Approval Expires 12/31/2000

4. What is Person 1's telephone number? *We may call this person if we don't understand an answer.*

Area Code + Number

5. What is Person 1's sex? *Mark* ☒ *ONE box.*
- ☐ Male ☐ Female

6. What is Person 1's age and what is Person 1's date of birth?

Age on April 1, 2000

Print numbers in boxes.

Month Day Year of birth

→ **NOTE: Please answer BOTH Questions 7 and 8.**

7. Is Person 1 Spanish/Hispanic/Latino? *Mark* ☒ *the* ***"No"*** *box if* ***not*** *Spanish/Hispanic/Latino.*
- ☐ **No,** not Spanish/Hispanic/Latino
- ☐ Yes, Puerto Rican
- ☐ Yes, Mexican, Mexican Am., Chicano
- ☐ Yes, Cuban
- ☐ Yes, other Spanish/Hispanic/Latino — *Print group.*

8. What is Person 1's race? ***Mark*** ☒ ***one or more races*** *to indicate what this person considers himself/herself to be.*
- ☐ White
- ☐ Black, African Am., or Negro
- ☐ American Indian or Alaska Native — *Print name of enrolled or principal tribe.*
- ☐ Asian Indian
- ☐ Japanese
- ☐ Native Hawaiian
- ☐ Chinese
- ☐ Korean
- ☐ Guamanian or Chamorro
- ☐ Filipino
- ☐ Vietnamese
- ☐ Samoan
- ☐ Other Asian — *Print race.*
- ☐ Other Pacific Islander — *Print race.*
- ☐ Some other race — *Print race.*

→ **If more people live here, continue with Person 2.**

The U.S. Census has been shortened to eight questions, to encourage participation. The 2000 questionnaire is shown above.

birth and death rates and migration, which, in turn, can be used to determine population change. These data can then be used to identify significant trends and patterns. Such information is particularly useful in determining future needs. The building of schools, hospitals, housing, transportation facilities, and many other services depends heavily on census data.

A much better idea of what census data can offer can be gained from the U.S. Census Bureau Home Page (www.census.gov). Much can be learned by browsing through the various links that appear by topic on the first page. A good place to begin is by accessing the "American FactFinder" that appears in the box at the upper left of the screen. Under "Fast Access to Information," enter your town or city, county, or ZIP code. As you will see, a world of information is available from the U.S. Census Bureau database.

WORLD POPULATION

In mid-2008, the world population stood at approximately 6.7 billion people. The number is growing by about 77 million people, or 1.2 percent, annually (assuming no change in the current rate of increase). Population, rates of natural increase, and life expectancy are not evenly distributed. Neither are rural and urban populations, population density, and income (see Figure 1).

Seventy-five percent of the world's population lives on two continents, Asia and Africa. Asia's population, however, is growing at the world average of 1.2 percent, whereas Africa's is growing at twice the rate, 2.4 percent. Africa is also the poorest of the continents. How will impoverished Africa be able to cope with a population estimated to double—to nearly 2 billion people—by 2040? Europe, on the other hand, is the first continent in modern times to have reached zero population growth (ZPG). Without immigrants, the continent's population will continue to become older and also decline in number.

Whereas figures such as those appearing in Figure 1 are interesting, they really are not that important. Human well-being, not

WORLD POPULATION BY CONTINENT

	Population [1]	Percent[2]	RNI[3]	Life exp.	% Urban	GNI/PPP[4]
WORLD	**6,686**	**100%**	**1.2%**	**68 yrs.**	**50%**	**$9,940**
Asia	4,058	61%	1.2%	68	41%	$6,630
Africa	967	14%	2.4%	53	37%	$2,550
Europe	732	11%	–0.1%	75	72%	$22,690
N. America	524	8%	*0.6%	*78	*79%	*$43,290
S. America	384	6%	**1.5%	*73	**76%	*$8,630
Australia	21	<1%	0.6%	81	91%	$31,860

[1] millions; [2] of world population; [3] annual rate of natural increase; [4] gross national income, purchasing power parity, or equivalent in U.S. buying power; *Indicates the United States and Canada; **indicates Latin America (Jan. 1, 2008 estimates)

[Data from various sources]

Figure 1

human numbers, is of greatest importance. This leads to the idea of "overpopulation" and the question "How many people is too many?" As you will see in the following section, this is not an easy question to answer!

OVERPOPULATION

"How many people can Earth support?" is a question that people have asked for centuries. In 1798, a British economist and clergyman, Thomas R. Malthus, published "An Essay on the Principle of Population. . ." He was concerned about what he believed to be a growing problem of overpopulation. People, he reasoned, increase geometrically ($2 \times 2 = 4 \times 2 = 8 \times 2 = 16$, etc.). Food, on the other hand, increases arithmetically ($1 + 1 = 2 + 1 = 3 + 1 = 4$, etc.). Malthus foresaw a time when population growth would surpass Earth's ability to feed its people. When this occurred, he believed, population growth would be checked by famine, disease, or war.

On the surface, Malthus's theory made sense to many people of the time. Yet Malthus and others failed to foresee some very important developments. Since his time, the human population has increased from about 900 million to some 6.7 billion, or by about seven and one-half times. Improvements in agriculture and food production, on the other hand, have far outstripped population growth. So have means of food preservation and distribution to places far distant from points of production. Nonetheless, since Malthus's time, many writers have sounded a "gloom-and-doom" alarm. They continue to believe that an out-of-control population explosion exists. Are they correct? The answer may surprise you.

There are many ways to measure human well-being. Obviously, were a condition of overpopulation to exist, humankind would be experiencing widespread suffering. Yet today, a greater percentage of the world's people are adequately fed, well nourished, healthy, and in other ways better off than at any previous time in human history. Life expectancy is longer than it has ever been. Massive famine has stalked humankind throughout most of history. Today, however, devastating famines resulting in hundreds of thousands or even millions of deaths simply do not occur.

To understand the "population dilemma"—the problems supposedly resulting from overpopulation—one must understand its causes. Surprisingly, perhaps, human well-being has very little to do with numbers of people. In defining overpopulation, most experts emphasize three factors. They cite numbers of people, population density, and the human condition, which they usually tie directly to crowding. Statistics, however, do not support their findings. Little if any relationship exists between population or population density and such indicators of well-being as per capita income, life expectancy, or the United Nations Human Development Index (HDI) rankings.

(continues on page 32)

MAKING CONNECTIONS

ANALYZING POPULATION DATA

Demographic data can reveal a great deal about a country. The figures presented here give only a glimpse of the kinds of information available. But even they reveal some striking differences between and among countries. Study the table and then consider the following questions:

- The world's 10 most populated countries account for nearly 4 billion people, or about 60 percent of the human population. What conclusions can you draw from the figures given? For example, do you see a pattern in annual RNI, life expectancy, urban population, per capita GDI-PPP, and HDI rankings?
- The United States and Japan stand out at one extreme in terms of GDI-PPP and their position on the HDI; Pakistan, Bangladesh, and Nigeria stand out at the other. Can you think of reasons that account for these differences?
- How many of the countries in the top 10 are located in the less developed world (LDCs)?
- Does a country's population necessarily contribute to its ranking as a world power? What factors can you think of that are more important than numbers of people alone in determining a country's place among other countries?
- If current rates of natural increase continue, will China still be the world's most populated country in mid-century? What country will replace it?

POPULATION BY COUNTRY (TOP 10)

	Pop (millions)	Annual[1] RNI	Years to double	Life exp.	% urban	Pop den mi/km	Per capita GDI-PPP[2]	HDI[3] ranking
1. China	1,330	0.6%	118	73	44%	357/138	$7,730	81
2. India	1,148	1.6%	44	69	28%	891/344	$3,800	128
3. U.S.A.	304	0.6%	117	78	79%	80/31	$44,260	12
4. Indonesia	232	1.4%	51	69	42%	316/122	$3,950	107
5. Brazil	189	1.4%	51	72	81%	57/22	$ 8,800	70
6. Pakistan	169	2.3%	31	62	34%	552/213	$2,500	136
7. Bangladesh	149	1.9%	37	62	23%	2,681/1,035	$2,340	140
8. Nigeria	144	2.5%	28	47	44%	404/156	$1,050	158
9. Russia	142	–0.5%	ZPG	65	73%	22/8	$11,620	67
10. Japan	128	0.0%	ZPG	82	79%	876/338	$33,730	8

[1] Rate of natural increase (based on births and deaths) is not to be confused with population increase or decline that is based upon both RNI and migration. The two figures may vary widely.

[2] Gross Domestic Income Purchasing Power Parity

[3] United Nations Human Development Index of human well-being based upon life expectancy, literacy, education, and standard of living.

Data from CIA World Factbook, current Population Reference Bureau Data Sheet, UN Human Development Index, and other sources.

(continued from page 29)

The author defines overpopulation as follows:

> Overpopulation is a condition in which the **culture** of a defined **population** and **area** is unable to **adequately provide** the **basic needs** of that population as determined by that culture's own established living **standards.**

Let's test the definition with a comparison of a very traditional culture and an advanced industrial nation. What land and resources are available to each of them? Can the traditional culture bring resources—food, fuel, and other supplies—from

The issue of overpopulation has less to do with sheer numbers than with quality of life. A crowded area might not be considered overpopulated if it can provide the basic needs and culture of its inhabitants. Unaffordable food, power shortages, and lack of clean water (as shown in the image of a village in Pakistan, above), even in an area that is not densely inhabited, can make a place overpopulated.

distant lands? How many natural resources within its own surroundings can it use? (Could the Eskimo, or Inuit, for example, use the petroleum and natural gas that lie beneath their land?) A developed country, on the other hand, imports much if not all of its many needs. Japan is the world's second-leading industrial power. Yet the island country must import 97 percent of all raw materials and natural resources used in its industries. It has the economic ability to make the entire world its food, raw material, and natural resource base.

Another factor that must be considered is culture. Different cultures have different needs. A traditional society may depend upon walking or a dugout canoe for moving about on land or water. How many ways do we travel on land, on water, and in the air? What different levels of technology and resource consumption are involved? Each culture establishes its own living standards, hence, its resource needs.

As you have seen, the primary factors that determine whether a condition of overpopulation exists within a country have little to do with numbers of people. Two important factors seem to account for much of the human suffering. First, most such countries are very poorly governed. Bad governments, in turn, contribute to poor economies. On the other hand, without exception, those countries with a strong, stable, democratic government and free market economy are quite well off. A poor government and a weak economy, rather than numbers of people, are the primary factors that determine whether a country is overpopulated.

GLOBAL CONNECTIONS

Have you heard the expression "A chain is no stronger than the weakest link"? In many respects, the same holds true in regard to the human population. Today, if people are suffering in one place, the global community responds. The annual flow of food and other aid from places of plenty to places of need amounts to billions of dollars. As the world becomes an increasingly "global" place, such exchanges will increase.

Humanitarian aid is but one of the many ways in which the world's population is interconnected. For example, in some areas of the world, including many LDCs, population is growing at a rapid pace. Elsewhere, as in many European countries (including Russia), population has begun to decline. One result of these conditions is the migration of millions of people, both legally and illegally, from poorer to richer countries (migration is the topic of Chapter 6). Today, we live in a closely linked global community. Demographic conditions in one area can and often do have a major impact on far distant lands and peoples.

POPULATION GROWTH AND CHANGE

During the past century, the human population has grown at a pace unrivaled in all of human history. So rapid has the growth occurred that it has been called a population "explosion." Obviously, this meteoric expansion in human numbers has caused widespread alarm among many concerned observers.

Outcries over rapid population growth and its consequences seem to have peaked about a half century ago. During the mid-1900s, the peril of uncontrolled population growth was a topic of widespread media exposure and heated debate. In its intensity, it rivaled today's frenzy over the global warming issue. At the time, the environment was, indeed, becoming increasingly polluted. Many nonrenewable resources were being consumed at a rapid and growing rate. Many social problems were being blamed on "urban crowding" and simply "more people" than Earth could support. Untouched natural landscapes were becoming scarce. People, it seemed, were everywhere. According to many experts, there were simply far too many of them.

The concerns of the time were mirrored in the titles of many books written on the subject. Some books focused upon population and the environment. Titles included *Road to Survival, The Rape of the Earth, Our Plundered Planet,* and *The Limits to Growth.* Books devoted primarily to population-related problems included *Our Crowded Planet, The Population Dilemma, Famine-1975!, The Population Bomb, Standing Room Only,* and *Population Crisis.*

When most of these books were written, nearly a half century ago, the human population was just above 3 billion, less than half what it is today. Yet during recent decades, population seems to have fallen by the wayside as a serious public concern. What happened? This chapter attempts to answer this question. As you read, be prepared for a number of surprises.

HOW POPULATIONS CHANGE

For the planet, only two factors can change population: births and deaths. For a particular location, however, in-migration and out-migration must be factored in, as well. In determining population change, demographers use the following formula, called the basic demographic equation:

Final population = + births – deaths + in-migration – out migration

Let's imagine a location with a beginning population of 1,000. During a year, there are (+) 14 births and (–) 5 deaths, (+) 26 in-migrants, and (–) 11 out-migrants. Have you figured its final population? If you did the math and determined it to be 1,024, you are right.

Rate of Natural Increase (RNI)

For any given population, the rate of natural increase (RNI) is determined by subtracting the crude death rate (CDR) from the crude birth rate (CBR). The CBR is the number of births per 1,000 population during a one-year period. Examples (2008 estimates) include:

Selected Crude Birth Rates (per 1,000)	
World	21
Less developed countries	27
More developed countries	11
Africa	41
Liberia and Guinea-Bissau	50
Europe	10
Germany	8
United States	14
Canada	11

The CDR is the number of deaths in one year per 1,000 people. Because the world population continues to grow, the CDR is considerably lower than the CBR. Sample figures (2008 estimates) include:

Selected Crude Death Rates (per 1,000)	
World	9
Less developed countries	8
More developed countries	10
Africa	14
Swaziland	29
Latin America	6
Kuwait, Qatar, UAE	2
United States	8
Canada	7

These figures may be surprising. Why, for example, do less developed countries have a lower crude death rate than developed lands? Why does Swaziland have such a high CDR, while Kuwait, Qatar, and the United Arab Emirates—all on the Arabian Peninsula—have such a low CDR? The answer to the first

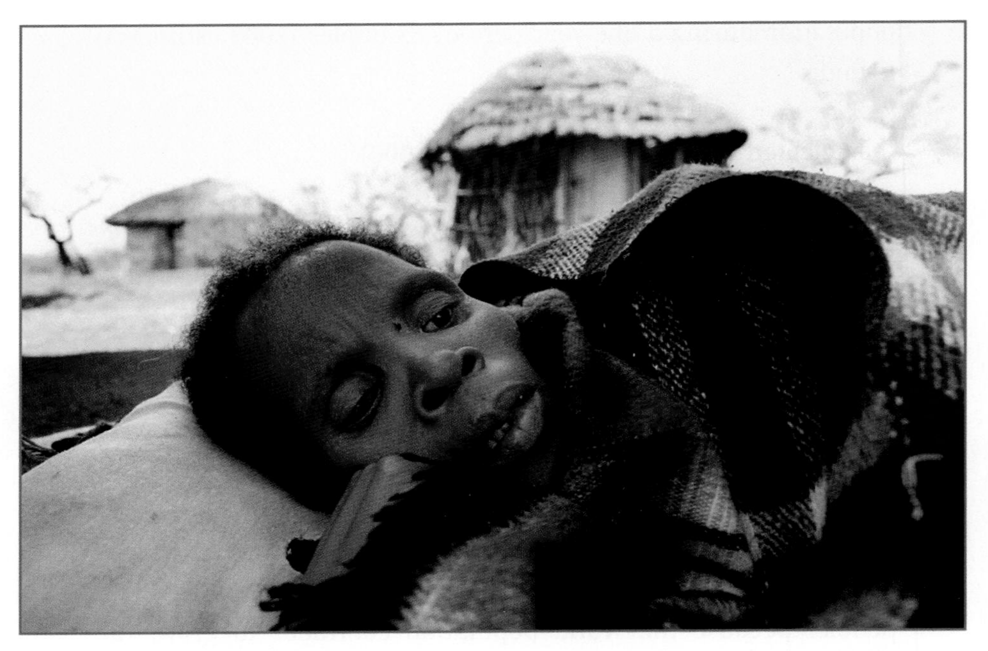

Disease and epidemics impact population rates. The crude death rate (CDR) is higher in countries like Swaziland in southern Africa, where AIDS occurrences are the highest in the world. Above, an AIDS sufferer rests outside her home near Magomba, Swaziland.

question can be found in the average age of the populations. Less developed countries (LDCs), on average, have a very young population (34 percent under 15 years of age vs. 17 percent in developed countries, or DCs). Developed countries, on the other hand, have a rapidly aging population (15 percent over 65 vs. only 5 percent in LDCs).

Swaziland's tragically high CDR is explained by the very high percentage of people who have HIV/AIDS. Nearly 26 percent of the population carries the often deadly disease. What about the incredibly low CDR in the three Arabian Peninsula countries? This is easily explained by the fact that up to 85 percent of the population is made up of young, generally healthy, immigrant males. They are drawn to these lands by jobs in the oil fields and booming construction industry.

The rate of natural increase is expressed as a percentage. It represents *natural* population growth or decline as determined by the number of births and deaths in a country during a one-year period. Sample figures including extremes (2008 estimates) include:

Selected Rates of Natural Increase	
World	1.2%
Less developed countries	1.8%
More developed countries	0.1%
Africa	2.4%
Niger	3.4%
Europe	–0.1%
Ukraine	–0.6%
United States	0.6%
Canada	0.3%

These figures clearly show that nearly all population growth is taking place in LDCs. In fact, today many developed countries—particularly those in Europe—are not reproducing themselves. Thirteen European countries, including Russia, Germany, and Poland, are actually experiencing a decline in their RNI. It is interesting to note that Africa leads the world in all three categories. The continent has the highest birth rates and the highest death rates. Because its CBR is so high, however, it also leads the world in the rate of natural increase. Many individual African countries are also clustered at the high end in each category.

Population Doubling Time

There is a simple formula for determining how long—based on current RNI figures—it will take for a country's population to double: divide 71 by its RNI. Africa, for example, has an RNI of 2.4 percent (71 ÷ 2.4 percent), giving a doubling time of just under 30 years (29.6). For the United States, with an RNI of 0.6 percent, the estimated doubling time is 118 years. How correct are these estimates? Many other factors must be considered. Most countries in Africa and Asia, for example, have little if any in-migration. The United States, on the other hand, receives hundreds of thousands (if not more) migrants each year. Many fac-

MAKING CONNECTIONS

DO YOU KNOW THAT . . .

- Perhaps the single most reliable indicator of human well-being is life expectancy. Today, the world figure stands at 68 years, an all-time high that has more than doubled since 1900 and continues to rise throughout most of the world.
- Hunger, malnutrition, and famine have plagued humankind throughout history. Today, fewer people—as a percentage of the human population—are hungry than ever before. Massive famines, which were commonplace as recently as the mid-twentieth century, are almost unknown now. There is ample food to go around.
- In a global cash-based economy, a country's per capita gross national product (GNP) and per capita income are good indicators of its people's ability to purchase goods and services. Many people fear that as population grows, there will be fewer capital resources (money and means of making wealth) to go around. Yet both figures stand at an all-time high. The world's people have never been better off financially.
- It seems reasonable to believe that as population grows, there will be less space for people to occupy, leading to severe crowding and its related problems. Because so many people are moving from the country to the city, more

tors can cause a country's population doubling time to increase or decrease dramatically from initial estimates.

Do Large Families Cause Poverty?

A country's rate of natural population increase is an important indicator of demographic, social, and economic conditions that affect its people. Regions with a low RNI generally share certain

unoccupied and underdeveloped land exists today than at any time in recent history. Rural population decline and land abandonment, in fact, has become a major economic problem in many countries, including the United States and Canada.

- A common line of thinking suggests that the human population is pushing toward a point at which the Earth will run out of natural resources. Some social scientists, however, believe that human beings are the planet's most important resource. As the population grows, new ways will be discovered to provide for human needs. Certainly, this has been the case throughout human history. There is no reason to believe that it will not continue.

Clearly, when we look about the world today, there are many problems. There are large pockets of hunger and widespread areas of grinding poverty. People in many lands are, indeed, extremely crowded. Yet are the problems related to "overpopulation"? Many social scientists believe not. They place the blame on human factors. Poverty and human hardship are only remotely related to population. These conditions are mainly the result of poor governments, rampant corruption, and noncompetitive economic systems. In order to solve a problem, one must understand its cause, and this certainly is true in regard to the population "crisis."

characteristics. For example, they experience a longer life expectancy and have a much higher per capita gross national income. This has contributed to a widely held belief that a direct relationship exists between population growth and economic well-being. This line of thinking holds that if population growth is slow, the economy will prosper. On the other hand, rapid population growth is a major contributor to poverty.

Actually, the exact opposite is true. Common sense suggests that if a location is prospering, people will be attracted to it and the population will grow. If an economy is weak, people will leave to seek better opportunities elsewhere.

In economically less developed countries, children are a very important economic resource to poor, rural families. Youngsters contribute to their family's economic well-being. They can fetch water, watch over flocks of livestock, and collect firewood. As adults, they provide care and often shelter for their elderly parents. These are just some of the reasons why families in LDCs are larger than those of developed lands.

Developed countries, on the other hand, have schooling requirements and child labor laws. Most jobs require knowledge and skills that take time and experience to gain. Urban youngsters need many costly items and receive many expensive services that are unknown to the rural poor. In the United States and Canada, the average cost of raising an urban child from birth to age 18 is more than $250,000! These are just some of the reasons why urban families are usually much smaller than those of country-dwelling people.

Are RNI and Population Change the Same?

Many people confuse a country's rate of natural increase (RNI) with its population growth rate. You must remember that RNI is based on *natural* population change. It is based solely on births and deaths. Actual population change includes migration. A country can actually have a negative RNI (that is, it has more deaths than births), but it will continue to grow in population as a result of in-migration. This condition is occurring in some West European countries today. Some countries, on the other hand, have a positive RNI, but they lose population because of even higher out-migration.

HISTORICAL POPULATION GROWTH

There are many different ways to show population growth through time. Only recently, of course, have actual data been available to document demographic changes. Calculating historical population changes involves a lot of guess work. Several things, however, are known with some certainty. Throughout perhaps 99 percent of human history, population grew at a very slow rate. Growth probably hovered around 1 percent each thousand years. Around the dawn of the Christian era, growth still occurred at a snail's pace, a few percent each century.

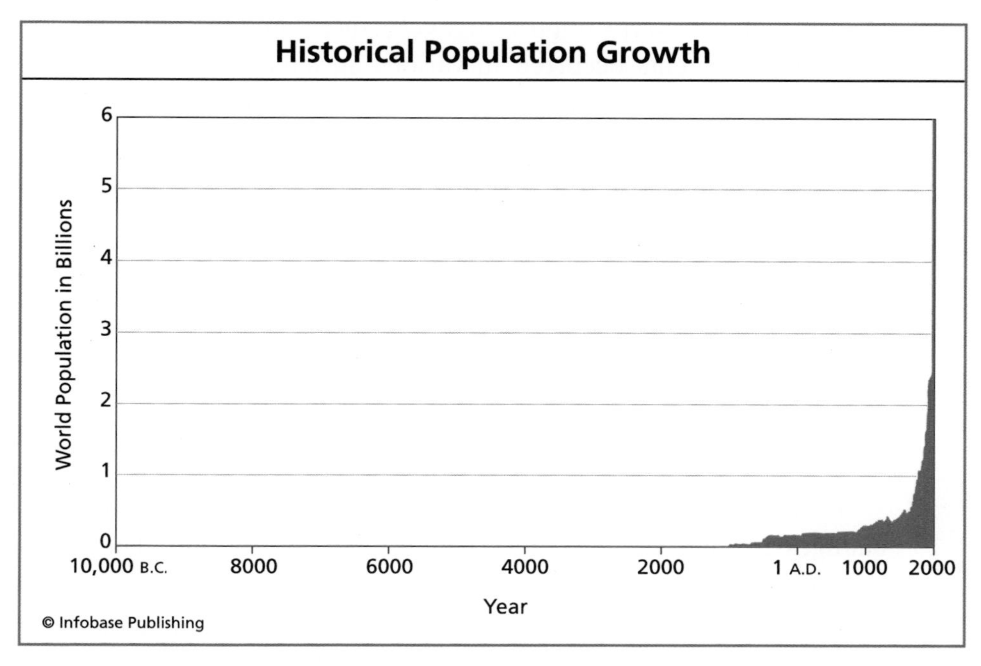

Figure 2

As is shown in Figure 2 on the previous page, population grew very slowly throughout most of history. High birth rates were offset by high death rates, resulting in very little gain in numbers. Life expectancy was short, perhaps no more than 20 years throughout most of human history. By the beginning of the Christian era, the RNI was about .06 percent each year. Around that time, farming methods began to improve. As this happened, the population began to grow in response to a growing food supply. By 1900, the population began to explode. During the 1970s, the RNI reached a non-sustainable all-time high of 2 percent each year. At that rate, the world population was on a pace to double every 35 years.

What happened to make this burst of population growth possible? Social scientists explain the change by pointing to several important cultural "revolutions." First, there was a huge revolution in food production. Technology made it possible to bring more land into production through the use of bigger and better farm equipment. Crops improved, greatly increasing their yields. Huge improvements occurred in various agricultural practices. The use of chemical fertilizers and more effective means of suppressing weeds and controlling insects boosted the food supply. So did fallowing fields (not raising a crop for a year), rotating crops, and increasing irrigation.

A second major revolution occurred in hygiene, medicine, and general health care. The causes of and cures for many previously fatal or debilitating diseases were discovered. Something as simple as the realization that germs can cause infections and diseases was a great step forward. So was the use of soap and other disinfectants to protect against them.

A third set of developments was related to revolutionary changes in food storage, preservation, and distribution. They combined to make it possible for more food to be available year-round. Food could also be easily distributed to many more people, including those living in cities and in distant needy places.

During the past three decades, the population "boom" has abruptly changed into what some experts now call the population "bust." Since the late 1970s, the RNI has dropped dramatically from 2.0 percent to the current 1.2 percent (some sources indicate 1.1 percent). The sharp drop is occurring in both developed and less developed countries.

FUTURE POPULATION

Social scientists often look to the past to forecast the future. They may, for example, base future estimates on past changes in various demographic data such as the CBR, CDR, and

Children work in a potato field in a village in India (above). In certain parts of the world, children are a tremendous resource to their families' economy. Kids in poor rural areas of underdeveloped countries are generally not required to attend school because they are believed to be much more useful as laborers and caregivers.

RNI. (Unless UFOs are bringing ETs to Earth, migration is not a factor for world population.) Many experts also look to society itself for changes that may provide clues to future populations.

Several things are known in regard to recent population change. First, between 1960 and 2008, a span of just 48 years, the population doubled from about 3.2 billion to 6.7 billion. At

THE DEMOGRAPHIC TRANSITION

The Demographic Transition model helps to explain the changes that occur in population growth as a society's culture changes. In its simplest form, it identifies four stages of development. Each stage links cultural development to population change. Birth and death rates appear in the vertical column; stages of economic development and population growth appear from left to right.

- Stage 1 is marked by high birth and death rates. Population changes slightly, but there is little growth. Economic activity and other aspects of culture are traditional. This is the stage in which humans existed throughout most of history. Today, only a few very remote people continue to exist in Stage 1.
- In Stage 2, death rates begin to drop in response to increased food production and improvements in hygiene and medicine. Birth rates, however, remain steady or even increase slightly. Populations begin to grow. In the West, this began with the Industrial Revolution around 1800.
- In Stage 3, death rates continue to drop at a sharp rate, and birth rates begin a slow decline. With many more births than deaths, and life expectancy greatly expanding because of improved medicine and hygiene, population soars.

the current 1.2 percent RNI, it would double again in 59 years (by 2067) to a whopping 13.2 billion. Yet most experts do not believe this will happen. United Nations (UN) demographers and many other population specialists paint a much more conservative picture. Most believe that the world population will top out at approximately 9 to 9.5 billion around 2050. It then will stabilize for a brief period and begin to decline.

In Stage 4, births and deaths begin to equalize, resulting in a stable population. When the two are equal, as is happening in much of the developed world, zero population growth (ZPG) is achieved. Any additional population growth must come from either an increase in the birth rate or from immigration.

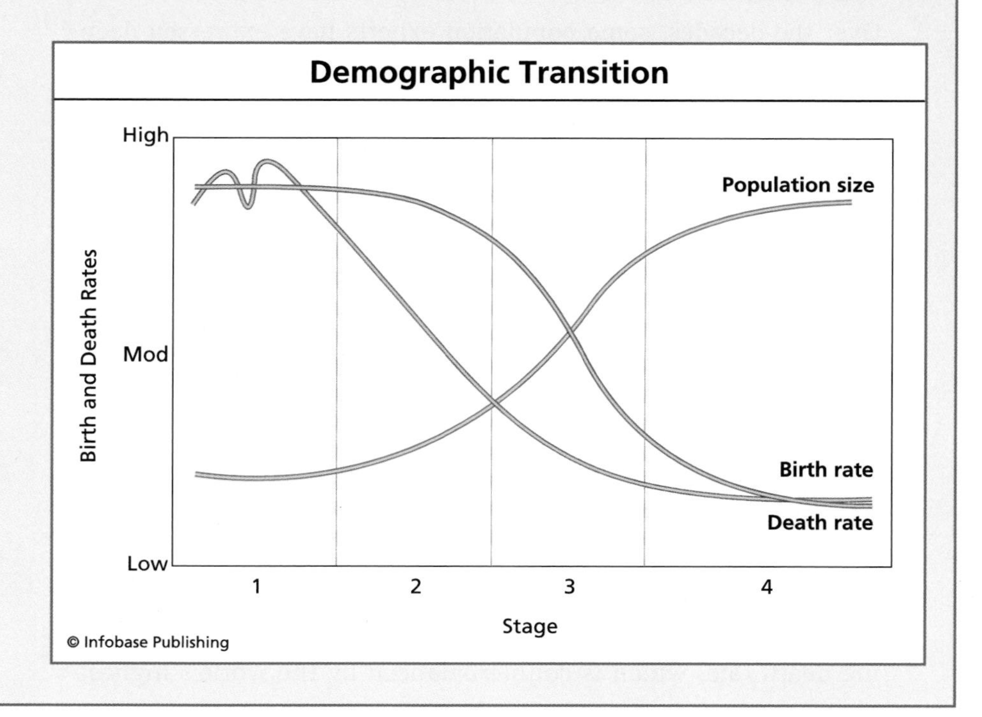

On what factors do these experts base this population projection? One very important clue is the sharp drop in the global RNI that has occurred during the past three decades. It has been reduced by almost half, from 2.0 percent to 1.2 percent. Many countries have reached or are approaching zero population growth (ZPG). Another important factor (discussed earlier) is that urban families have fewer children. In fact, nearly all urban growth is the result of in-migration rather than natural increase. During recent decades, urban populations have risen sharply. By 2009, half of the world's people lived in cities. In Europe, Latin America, Northern America, and Australia, 75 to 90 percent of the population is urban. As people in LDCs continue to flock to cities, they will begin to have fewer children and smaller families. This will cause a sharp drop in the RNI.

POPULATION AND HUMAN WELL-BEING

Over the decades, some population experts have expressed deep concern about the relationship between a growing population and a feared decline in human well-being. As they see it, there are simply too many people. They see the Earth's resources, agricultural production, jobs, and other necessities as being finite (limited). As the population grows, they reason, there will be less and less to go around. Humans will suffer as a result. Has this happened? See the sidebar on page 46 to determine if these people were right.

A REGIONAL OVERVIEW

As you have seen throughout this book, huge demographic differences exist from region to region. Africa's population, for example, continues to grow at the explosive annual rate of 2.4 percent. This growth is achieved despite the continent's staggering death rate, which is counterbalanced by the world's highest birth rate. Europe, on the other hand, now has a negative rate of natural increase. Without in-migration, the continent's population will continue to decline. In fact, today most of the economically developed world is approaching ZPG.

Because of its huge numbers—61 percent of the world's population—what happens in Asia has a major effect on demographic statistics. During recent decades, the continent has seen a sharp decline in its RNI. Today, it stands at 1.2 percent, identical to the current world average. A half century ago, Latin America had the world's highest RNI, a staggering 2.9 percent growth each year. As the culture realm has urbanized, industrialized, and become better educated, its rate of population growth has dropped dramatically. Today, the region's population is increasing at a rate of 1.5 percent, only slightly above the world average.

The United States and Canada continue to have rates of natural increase that contribute to growing populations in both countries. In-migration, however, rather than RNI, is responsible for most population growth in these Northern American lands. The United States and its northern neighbor will continue to attract immigrants. So will most other economically developed countries with aging populations. In these lands, nearly all population growth will result from immigration of peoples from LDCs.

MAKEUP OF THE POPULATION

Populations differ greatly. Their composition, or makeup, includes many different kinds of people. Obviously, there are males and females. Some are younger and others are older. And both race (biological inheritance) and ethnicity (culture, or learned way of life) can differ greatly. The same holds true for literacy, the ability to read and write in one's language. In a society that values tolerance and diversity, these differences may seem unimportant. Yet they can be of great significance, depending upon other conditions. This chapter discusses these differences and their importance.

SEX RATIO

The most basic measure of population composition is the sex ratio, the proportion of males to females. It is determined by a simple formula. The number of males in a population is divided by the number of females, and the quotient, or resulting number, is multiplied by 100. For example, based upon the 2000 census, the U.S. sex ratio was:

$$\textbf{Sex ratio} = \frac{138{,}053{,}563 \text{ (males)}}{143{,}368{,}343 \text{ (females)}} = .963 \times 100 = \mathbf{96.3}$$

What does this number mean? A ratio of 100 indicates that a population is composed of an equal number of males and females. If the ratio is above 100, there are more males than females. For example, at birth the sex ratio is 105. This means that 105 male babies are born for every 100 female births. This appears to be nature's way of equalizing sexes. For various reasons, infant mortality (infant death) is higher among males than females. As the population reaches young adulthood, figures tend to even out. A sex ratio below 100 indicates that there are more females than males. In the United States, according to the 2000 census, there were 96.3 men for every 100 women.

Worldwide, the sex ratio is 100.5, indicating an almost even number of males and females. Yet the proportion varies greatly from place to place and even time to time. Young men, for example, are much more apt to move to frontier areas than are women. During the mid-nineteenth-century gold rush, California's sex ratio was 1223–12 men for each woman! Can you imagine some of the social problems that imbalance created! When Alaska's oil boom began in the early 1970s, thousands of young men flocked to the state. Many of them found high-paying jobs working on the Alaska pipeline. The state had and continues to have the nation's highest sex ratio. The same holds true for the present-day tar sand oil boom in northern Alberta, Canada.

Worldwide, the highest sex ratios are in the oil-rich Middle East. In fact, of the nine countries with a sex ratio of 105 or more, all of them are in Southwest Asia. The reason for the high number of males is jobs. Oil fields, oil refineries, and the region's booming construction industry all offer employment. The jobs attract hundreds of thousands of workers, most of whom come

The sex ratios in the Middle East are the highest in the world. This is due in large part to the types of jobs available in that region. The ratio is illustrated in the above photo, which shows a shopping mall in Dubai, United Arab Emirates. Note that there are no females in the crowd.

from poor South Asian countries like India, Pakistan, or Bangladesh. In the United Arab Emirates, there are 186 males to every 100 females. Qatar and Kuwait fall close behind with 173 and 151, respectively.

Most of the lowest sex ratios are in Russia and several former Soviet republics. There, the male life expectancy has dropped by nearly 10 years since the fall of the USSR in 1991. Excessive smoking and drinking, stress, suicide, and other lifestyle decisions have caused the male death rate to soar. Estonia and Latvia both have a sex ratio of 85, followed closely by Lithuania, Ukraine, and Russia with 87. This part of the world also experienced millions of male deaths during World War II. This took a terrible toll on males who would now be in their eighties had they lived.

A population imbalance of sexes can cause problems. Some are easily understood. In California's gold fields, for example, it would have been all but impossible for a man to find a Saturday night date! Some are more serious. Statistically, for example, males are much more apt than females to commit violent crimes. One of the greatest problems related to sex ratios is found in southern and eastern Asia. In China and rural India, for example, culture plays a dominant role in determining the sex ratio. China's 2000 census resulted in a sex ratio of 117, far above the normal average. In some provinces, the ratio soared to above 135. How can China's strange sex imbalance be explained?

Some social scientists have referred to the men who outnumber women in China as bare branches. The reference is to trees (families) with no leaves (females) on some branches (males). To understand the importance of bare branches, we must understand Chinese culture. In China and other Asian countries, males are preferred. At marriage, for example, it is the custom for the husband's family to receive a dowry (a payment in cash or material gifts) from the wife's family. This can impose a huge financial burden on families with only girls. Additionally, after marriage most brides become socially and economically tied to the husband's family, resulting in a further financial loss. Traditionally, males also have had the responsibility of caring for their elderly parents.

In 1980, because of China's explosive rate of natural population increase at the time, the government imposed a one-child policy. Families that had a single child received many benefits. Those having more than one child, however, were severely punished. It is here that technology plays an important role. By the 1980s, ultrasound was well developed. It is a method by which the sex of a fetus (unborn child) can be determined. For reasons explained above, it is very important in Chinese culture to have a boy. Yet the Chinese government imposed a one-child rule. Therefore, if the unborn fetus is female, many families simply decide on abortion.

China's sex imbalance has resulted in a tremendous social problem. Today, the country has about 40 million bare branches: young men of marrying age for whom there are no women. This number becomes more meaningful when one compares populations. Forty million is about 7 million more people than live in all of Canada, or 4 million more than live in California, the most populated state in the United States.

AGE STRUCTURE

The age distribution of a population is extremely important for any country or society. Have you ever heard or read a refer-

MAKING CONNECTIONS

AGING POPULATIONS

Many of the world's countries either have reached or are approaching zero population growth (ZPG). Nearly all such lands are economically well developed. They include much of Europe including Russia, the United States and Canada, Japan, and Australia. As the rate of natural increase (RNI) declines, two things happen. First, the population begins to decline if the loss is not offset by in-migration. Second, a country's population ages because there are fewer births.

Is achieving ZPG good or bad? What happens when a country's population begins to decline? Many people, after all, believe that population decline is a good thing. But is it for everyone? Does everyone agree?

An aging population can create many problems. Senior citizens require more health care and medical attention. Rather than paying into retirement programs, they begin to withdraw pensions. In the United States, the Social Security program, according to many

ence to baby boomers, or perhaps Generation X (or Y)? They are examples of what demographers call *age cohorts,* or groups of people who form a population age group. In the United States, for example, age groups, by year of birth, are as follow:

Date of birth	Generation
1914–1932	World War II generation
1933–1945	Silent generation
1946–1964	Baby boomers
1965–1977	Generation X
1978–1994	Generation Y
1995–present	Millennial generation

experts, will be bankrupt by 2018. It will then pay out more money than it takes in. Additionally, a great number of jobs go begging in search of people willing or able to do them. Many of these are entry-level positions that pay low wages. With an aging population, who will fill them? At the other extreme, some positions require extensive training and highly specialized skills. Who will fill these positions as retirees leave the workforce?

The answer to the problem of a declining and aging population is simple: increased migration. Today, many millions of people, particularly those from LDCs, are migrating in search of employment. Many are willing to take jobs that cannot (or will not) be filled by the domestic population. Others are well educated and highly skilled. Both groups boost a country's economy in many ways. Further, they add to the richness of a country's cultural diversity. Of greatest importance, perhaps, is the fact that they have become absolutely essential to the economy of many lands. As you can see, for many countries and for most immigrants, migration is a win-win situation.

Why is grouping people by age cohorts important? Social scientists have long realized that each age group is unique. People of a particular age group tend to think, buy, and act in ways that differ from other age groups. Each cohort has its own particular interests and needs. Do you, for example, share the same thoughts, buy the same things, and dress and act in the same way as your teachers, parents, or grandparents? The age distribution of its population can have a major impact on a region. It affects its economy, political outlook, social interactions, and needed services.

Young people have certain needs and behaviors when compared to the elderly. They are, for example, more apt to be in school and participate in sports activities than are the elderly. They seek entry-level jobs and have relatively low disposable incomes. Younger adults are more apt to marry, start families, and buy or rent "starter" homes. They also are much less tied to place, hence, more apt to move. In terms of behavior, they also take more chances, are more impulsive, and are more prone to violence than the elderly. As a result, young people are involved in more motor vehicle accidents and commit more crimes.

Age structure can be influenced by many factors. In the United States and Canada, many old, decaying industrial cities have aging populations. So do many states and provinces located in the "heartland" of each country. This can be explained by the out-migration of young people. Young people tend to flee economically depressed regions. Most go elsewhere in search of employment. They are attracted to areas that are prospering. Many cities, for example, offer attractive employment options and many other attractive opportunities and amenities.

Some counties and communities in the United States have startling high average ages. Such areas often are those that attract a large number of retirees. Sun City, Arizona, a Phoenix suburb, is a classic example (see Figure 3). Areas with older populations have many specific needs. These include retirement

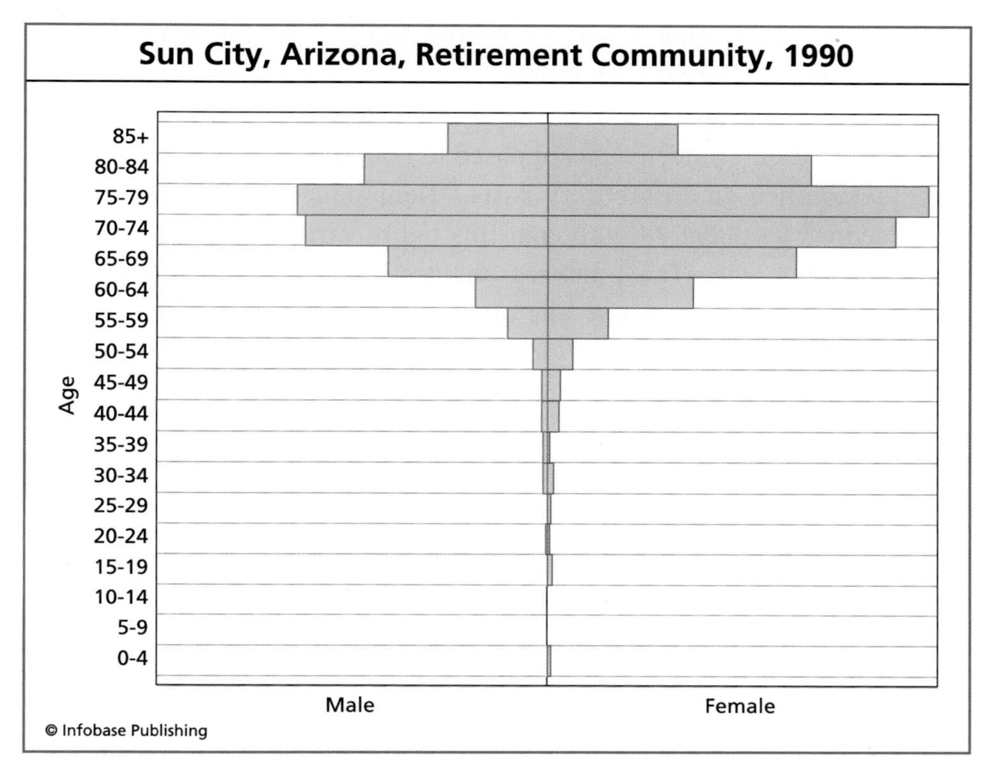

Figure 3

and long-term health care centers. The elderly are also attracted to the types of restaurants, recreational opportunities, shopping, and entertainment not usually associated with younger people.

THE DEPENDENCY RATIO

Have you ever heard someone complain about the money problems that the U.S. Social Security system faces? The dependency ratio can help you better understand what is happening to cause a future financial crisis within the program. In simple terms, America's population is aging rapidly. In 1945, 42 workers were paying into the Social Security program for each retiree. Today the figure has dropped to three workers. By the time most baby boomer generation people are retired, the ratio will drop to two workers to support each retiree.

The dependency ratio is a way of showing how many people are in their productive, as opposed to nonproductive, years. It is determined on an arbitrary basis. "Nonproductive" is normally defined as under 18 (although this figure varies from 15 to 20) and 65 or older. This number is divided by the population in the 18 to 64 year age group. The quotient is then multiplied by 100 to give the ratio. Using this formula, the dependency ratio for the United States based upon the 2000 census data was:

281,000,000 **total population**
– 72,000,000 **nonproductive**
209,000,000 **productive**

$$\textbf{Dependency ratio } \frac{72{,}000{,}000}{209{,}000{,}000} = .345 \times 100 = \mathbf{34.5}$$

In other words, in 2000, the United States had 100 people working to support every 35 dependent people, those younger than 18 or 65 and older. Again, the figure is arbitrarily determined. Many young people hold jobs, as do an increasing number of people over 65.

As a general rule, dependency ratios are highest in less developed countries (LDCs) and lowest in Western industrial/urban societies. In LDCs, the high figure results from the fact that a very high percentage of the population is under 18. The Population Reference Bureau (PRB) uses birth to under 15 years and 65 years or older to determine age breakdowns. According to PRB (2007) data, 28 percent of the world population is under 15 and 7 percent is over 65. These figures, however, vary greatly from region to region.

In the less developed world (minus China), 34 percent of the population is younger than 15 and only 5 percent is 65 or older. In Uganda, where the annual RNI is 3.1 percent, 50 percent of the population is under 15. In the more developed world, only 17 percent of the population is under 15. Yet many people live long lives, resulting in 16 percent of the population being over 65 years of age. As a region, Europe has the lowest percentage of young people and the highest percentage of elderly. Population pyramids are a way of visualizing a country's sex and age distributions.

POPULATION PYRAMIDS

A population pyramid is a diagram that shows a country's population makeup by male and female and the percent of the population in various age groups. The diagram has two side-by-side horizontal bar graphs, one for males and one for females. This makes it possible for one to see what percentage of the population is male or female within a particular age group.

Most developing countries have a very young population. This is indicated by the wide base of the pyramid (see Figure 4). Just over 18 percent of the entire population is in the 0–4 year age group. Because many LDCs have a shorter life expectancy, there are very few elderly people.

The population pyramid in Figure 5 is typical of that for a developed country. It is narrow at the base, indicating a low birth rate and few younger people. In the middle, it is quite wide, indicating a large middle-aged population. The pyramid stays quite wide all the way to the top, indicating a large number of elderly people.

Population pyramids for all the world's countries can be found on the U.S. Census Bureau Web site: http://www.census.gov/ipc/www/idb/pyramids.html.

You might want to begin by comparing population pyramids for Mali and Niger with those of Russia and Ukraine. What ideas can you draw from the pyramids for the United States and Canada? Compare the pyramids for the United States and Mexico. Do they provide a hint why so many Mexicans come to the United States?

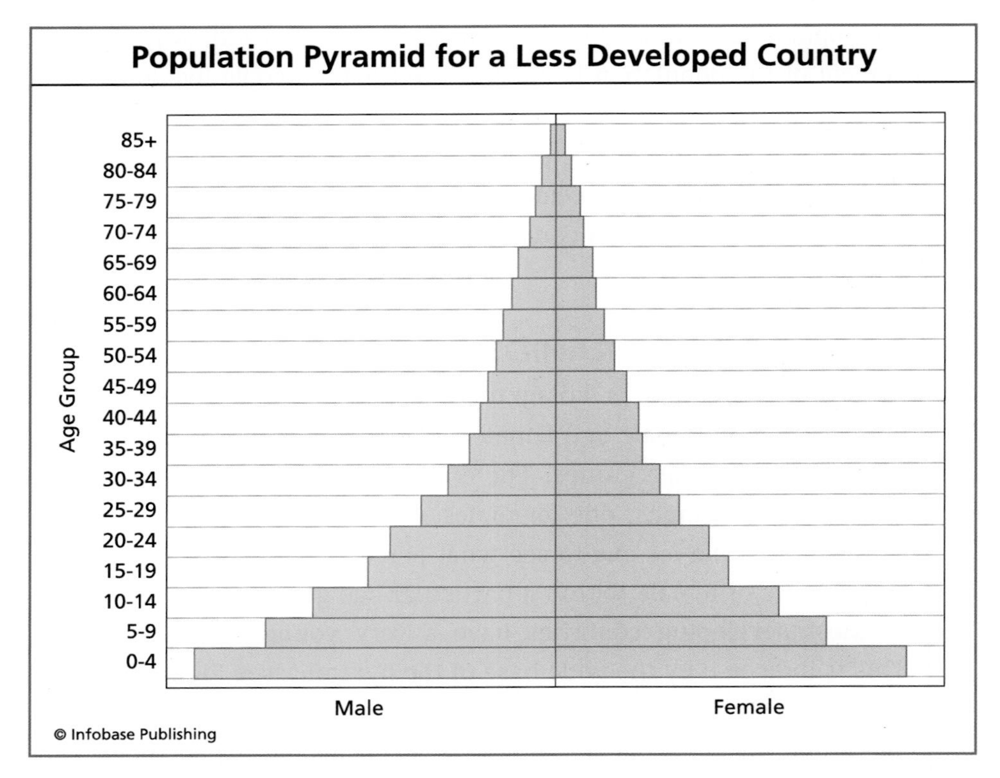

Figure 4

LITERACY

Literacy is defined as the percentage of a country's people over age 15 that is able to read and write. It is perhaps the single most important indicator of a country's economic development and the well-being of its people. Most countries in the more developed world have literacy rates of 99 percent. (In any large population, there will be a small number of people who, for various reasons, are unable to develop reading and writing skills.)

As you would expect, all lands with low literacy rates are LDCs. Fifteen of the 18 countries with a literacy rate below 50 percent are in Africa. When a country's population is largely illiterate, it is very difficult to govern democratically. In today's service-oriented global economy, people must be well educated

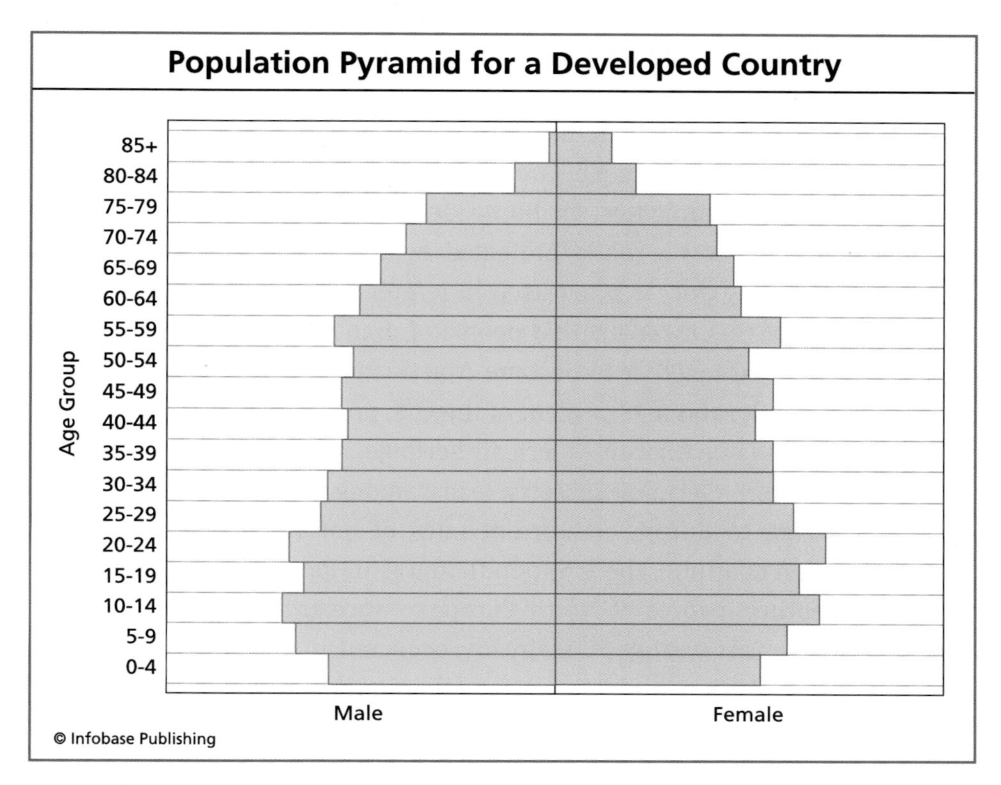

Figure 5

to succeed. Literacy, government, and economy are very closely interrelated. For example, it is difficult if not impossible for a country's economy to develop if many of its people are illiterate. If a country is poor, it will be unable to provide an adequate education for all of its citizens.

Today, the global economy is changing rapidly. Most developed countries no longer depend upon a "blue collar" labor force. Jobs in agriculture, lumbering, fishing, mining, and heavy manufacturing have dwindled. The economy of developed countries is "postindustrial." That is, it is based upon providing various services. Most service industries, such as health care, banking, education, tourism, media, and sales, require a literate workforce. Literacy, therefore, is a key to a country's economic success.

RACE AND ETHNICITY

Many populations are also divided by people of different racial (biological) and ethnic (cultural) backgrounds. The United States and Canada, for example, are home to people of all races and hundreds of ethnicities. In both countries, people of all backgrounds are now equally protected by constitutional law. The term "melting pot" is often used in reference to the U.S. population. What this means is that people of many races and cultures have blended together to become Americans.

Currently, about 13 percent of the U.S. population is Hispanic, 12 percent is of African-American heritage, and 3.6 percent is of Asian origin. German ancestry leads among those whose roots trace back to Europe. If current rates of natural increase and migration continue, the U.S. population is in for a big change. By mid-century, people of North European ancestry will become a minority. This change has already occurred in Hawaii, California, New Mexico, and Texas. Canada, too, has a rich racial and ethnic diversity of people.

GLOBAL CONNECTIONS

In an ideal world, all people—based upon sex, age, and heritage—would be considered and treated as equals. Unfortunately, this is not the case. In many of the world's current hot spots, flames of hatred rage between people of different backgrounds. Millions of lives have been lost in such conflicts. Central Africa, Sudan, the Balkans (the former Yugoslavia), and Iraq are four of many areas in which ethnic cleansing has occurred recently. This is an attempt by one or more groups to destroy another.

In today's global community, conflict in one place can have a great impact on other distant locations. The United States and its allies, for example, are deeply involved in the Middle East. In both Iraq and Afghanistan, much of the strife is based upon clashes between different ethnic, tribal, and religious groups.

Elsewhere, more than 150 countries have accepted refugees, most of whom are escaping ethnic-based conflicts.

During coming decades, one of the world's major demographic shifts will be a continued decline in the rate of population increase. This, in turn, will cause a "population bust," fewer young people and a rapidly aging population. As is explained in Chapter 6, this situation could pose a huge economic threat to all developed countries. The solution, of course, is in-migration. In both the United States and Canada, this solution has already changed the makeup of the population. It will continue to do so.

POPULATION DENSITY AND DISTRIBUTION

Few images are more revealing than that of the world at night as seen from distant space. Here and there, areas of bright light appear as islands in a sea of darkness. Brightly illuminated areas are densely settled. Here, millions of people live tightly packed in huge cities, closely spaced towns, and dense rural settlements. Much of the map, however, has only small and widely scattered spots of light. Some areas are completely dark. These patches of light and darkness reveal where people live and those areas they avoid.

Population distribution and density can tell us a great deal about people, society, and culture ("way of life"). Social scientists refer to these conditions as *settlement patterns*. This chapter focuses upon human settlement, with emphasis on the distribution and density of population. It attempts to explain why people cluster in some areas and avoid others. Finally, it investigates changing patterns of settlement and how they affect people and places throughout much of the world.

POPULATION DENSITY

If a social scientist could select only a single map to use in teaching, what would it be? Many would choose a world map showing population distribution and density. Look closely at the "World at Night" map. Can you explain some of the areas of dense light? What about areas of darkness? Geographers, demographers, and others attempt to understand why such patterns exist. They seek to explain why millions of people flock to some areas, while other regions are largely avoided. Their task is not easy. Some deserts, wet tropical areas, and mountainous regions have very few people. Yet elsewhere, almost identical environments are densely packed with people.

Population density refers to the number of people living within a defined area, such as a square mile or square kilometer.

This is a map of the world at night. The image is a composite of hundreds of pictures taken by orbiting satellites. Human-made lights highlight the populated areas of Earth's surface. The darkest areas are the sparsely inhabited portions of the world.

As of 2008, the world population density was approaching 130 persons per square mile (50 per sq km). A population density map clearly reveals that such information is extremely misleading. People are not evenly distributed about Earth's surface. Some areas, such as much of Antarctica and the Greenland ice cap, support no population. In other areas, people are tightly packed. Tiny Monaco, on the Mediterranean coast of France, has a density of about 40,000 people per square mile (16,760 per sq km).

IS THERE A RELATIONSHIP BETWEEN POPULATION DENSITY AND HUMAN WELL-BEING?

Many people believe that a close connection exists between population density and human well-being. They suggest that as the density increases, so do problems resulting from too many people and too much crowding. In this scenario, there simply is not enough space or opportunity to "go around." The standard of living, they reason, is threatened. With so many people, poverty, crime, and hunger may increase. So may numerous other social problems. The natural environment may be pressed to its limits.

Those who support this theory often point to places such as Bangladesh as an example. The poor, crowded South Asian country has a population density of about 2,750 people per square mile (1,070 per sq km). Its per capita GDP-PPP is about $1,400. (GDP-PPP measures the purchasing power of different currencies over comparable goods and services). But do the data support this belief? Is there any relationship between population density and a peoples' standard of living? See for yourself by looking at the chart on the right.

What do these figures tell us? Certainly they suggest that no relationship exists between numbers of people, population density, wealth, and quality of life. Yet they tell us more. They provide a clue to perhaps the single most important factor determining whether a country and its people prosper or struggle: good government versus

In very few countries do population density figures tell the real story. In fact, worldwide about 90 percent of the population lives on only some 10 percent of the land. About 90 percent of all Egyptians, for example, live in the narrow Nile River Valley. In Russia and China, huge areas of each country are all but uninhabited. The same holds true for Brazil and Canada. In the United States, 75 percent of the population lives in only 2 percent of the land area. Densities are very low in much of the interior central and western United States and in much of Alaska.

poor government. Can you identify those countries that have stable democratic governments and a free market economy? Can you spot those that are poorly governed and have a weak economy?

Country	Density mi^2 / km^2	GDP-PPP
Iceland	8 / 3	$39,400
Canada	7 / 3	$38,200
Australia	7 / 3	$31,860
Guyana	9 / 4	$5,300
Mongolia	4 / 2	$2,900
Mauritania	6 / 3	$1,800
Luxembourg	1,026 / 430	$80,000
Singapore	24,590 / 6,369	$48,900
Netherlands	942 / 395	$38,600
Haiti	1,040 / 307	$1,900
Bangladesh	1,045 / 2,494	$1,400
Rwanda	820 / 343	$1,000

Data from CIA World Factbook and other sources

WHERE PEOPLE LIVE AND WHY

Ancient Greeks had a word for the inhabited world. They called it the *ecumene*. To the Greeks, the ecumene was a relatively small area. They believed that humans could not live in the hot, humid "Torrid Zone." They also thought that civilization could never exist in the far northern "Frigid Zone." Today, of course, most of Earth's land surface is inhabited. Yet the distribution of population certainly is unequal. People, after all, have basic needs. They must have food, water, and shelter to protect them from the elements. They also must be able to make an adequate living in some way. Some accomplish this by farming or raising livestock. Others hold wage-paying jobs in resource-producing or manufacturing industries. Today, a growing number of people make their living by providing services to others. In some areas, it is very easy to make a living; in others, it is very difficult. Such conditions are reflected in population densities.

Many technological developments through time have helped humans greatly expand the ecumene. Better housing, artificial heating, and warm clothing offer protection against the cold. Today, hundreds of millions of people live comfortably in bone-chilling environments. Technology has also made life possible in many deserts. Deep wells, huge dams and reservoirs, and massive water transfer schemes have brought water to many otherwise parched environments. They have turned unproductive desert landscapes into productive agricultural regions. In many desert regions, including the southwestern United States, populations have boomed. Effective refrigerated air-conditioning was developed about 50 years ago. In the United States, it helped the hot "Sun Belt" become the country's fastest-growing region during the last half century.

Technology also makes it possible to move natural resources, raw materials, and finished products from place to place. Many areas lack adequate energy resources, sufficient food, or other essential supplies. Yet if adequate capital resources (such as money) are available, these needs can be filled through trade. In this way, global connections help people survive in places where living might otherwise be difficult.

Oceans cover 71 percent of Earth's surface. Here and there, widely scattered islands support populations that are generally low. Oceania is home to fewer than 40 million people. Most of the world's people live on the continental landmasses or on nearby islands such as Japan, Great Britain, or the islands of Indonesia. Yet even on land, populations tend to be quite clustered:

- 50 percent of the world's population lives in 5 percent of the land area
- 90 percent of the world's people live on 10 percent of the land area
- 90 percent of the world's population lives in the Northern Hemisphere
- 90 percent of the world's population lives in the "Land Hemisphere" (the half of Earth's surface that contains 85 percent of all land) centered on an area near Nantes, France
- 70 percent of the world's population lives within 600 miles (965.6 km) of saltwater
- 80 percent of the world's population lives below an elevation of 1,640 feet (500 m)
- 56 percent of the world's population lives below an elevation of 656 feet (200 m)
- 61 percent of the world's population lives in Asia
- 50 percent of the world's population is rural and 50 percent is urban
- 53 percent of the U.S. population lives in counties facing the Atlantic or Pacific ocean

A population map shows concentrations of population in the following environments:

- Fertile coastal plains
- Fertile interior and river valley plains

- Some humid tropical areas
- Many moist temperate regions
- Arid regions with fertile soils and available water for domestic use and irrigation
- Areas affected by the Industrial, Commercial, and Post-Industrial (service-oriented) revolutions

Highly productive agriculture explains dense population clusters in much of eastern, southeastern, and southern Asia. Well-developed industry and commerce explains concentrations in Western Europe, portions of the United States, Japan, and scattered urban areas elsewhere. A mix of agriculture and industry explains most other population clusters.

PLACES WITH FEW PEOPLE

As a general rule, population declines with increased latitude, elevation, and distance from the sea. It also drops sharply where agricultural production is limited or where wage-paying jobs are few. In explaining those places in the world that support low population densities, the "too lands" idea is useful. These are places that in some way are too extreme to be easily developed. They may be too hot or too cold, too wet or too dry, too high and rugged, or too remote. Some lands, for example, are too cold. Severe temperatures are difficult and costly to protect against. Such areas may have few food resources. Transportation is difficult, and permafrost (permanently frozen layer belowground) makes construction difficult and costly. Many deserts are too dry. They lack adequate water resources to support much settlement and development.

Hot, wet, tropical areas often discourage settlement. In some places, diseases and parasites limit the population. Dense rain forests are difficult to penetrate. Most tropical soils are heavily leached of their nutrients and are infertile. Heavy rains result in many streams that make land transportation very difficult and costly. Rugged terrain limits access and adds greatly to the cost of building and travel. Agriculture is difficult on steep slopes (unless, of course, they are terraced).

All "too lands," however, offer exceptions. Mineral exploitation, for example, has drawn people into even the harshest environments. So have strategic military and administrative activities. Today, scientific research and tourism have boosted populations in many formerly remote and desolate lands.

CHANGING SETTLEMENT PATTERNS

Settlement patterns change constantly. A half century ago, who could have guessed that the United States was on the brink of a massive shift in population? The Northeast and its once thriving industrial cities suddenly became a region of massive outmigration. Hundreds of industries and millions of people fled the northeastern "Rust Belt" or "Snow Belt." They moved to the much warmer "Sun Belt" of the South and Southwest.

Booming Cities

Worldwide, the greatest change in settlement is the explosive growth of cities. As urban centers grow, rural populations often decline. Huge cities began to grow in response to the Industrial Revolution. With industries came jobs. People working in manufacturing, in turn, required numerous services. They needed food, clothing, shelter, and services such as schools, transportation, and health care. In 1801, London, England, became the world's first industrial center with a population of one million people. As France industrialized, Paris soon followed.

In 2009, for the first time in history, one-half of the world's people lived in urban centers. In developed countries, about 75 percent of the population is urban. In less developed lands, about 40 percent of the people live in cities. Nearly eight of every ten people in the United States and Canada live in metropolitan areas. Australia, where 91 percent of the people live in cities, is the most urbanized continent. The least urbanized is Africa, where only 37 percent of the population lives in cities.

People are attracted to cities for many reasons. First and foremost, cities are where the "action" is. They offer hundreds of kinds of wage-paying jobs. Better health care, sanitation facilities, education, and countless other services are available. They also offer greater options for shopping and entertainment.

Two centuries ago, about 3 percent of the world's people lived in cities. Today, half of the population is urban. According to UN estimates, by 2030, some 60 percent of all people will reside in cities. In 1950, 83 cities had a population of one million or more. Today the number is approaching 500.

According to UN data, only five cities had a population of more than 10 million in 1975. Three of them were in the less developed world. Today, an estimated 25 megacities have a metropolitan population of 10 million or more. All but five of them (Tokyo, New York, Los Angeles, London, and Paris) are in less developed countries (LDCs).

Attempts to determine a city's population can be somewhat maddening. A half dozen "reliable" sources may give six different population figures. For example, according to census data figures, the population of New York City is about 8.2 million. The UN, on the other hand, lists a figure of 17.8 million. Still other sources indicate a population of nearly 30 million for the city. Huge differences such as these can be found for most cities. Why? The answer lies in the definition of "city."

Lower-range figures usually refer to the city proper. This is the area under the political jurisdiction (control) of that city. Yet most cities have suburbs that extend far into the surrounding area. This is a city's urban or metropolitan area. When surrounding populations are included in the count, much higher figures result.

Experts seem to agree that the Tokyo-Yokohama metropolitan area, with 30-plus million people, is the world's largest urban area. Such figures are, of course, difficult to grasp. Let's look at it another way. Within an area the size of a typical U.S. county,

MAKING CONNECTIONS

THE GROWING URBAN WORLD

The World's Megacities

Tokyo, Japan (33.8 million)
Seoul, South Korea (23.9 million)
Mexico City, Mexico (22.9 million)
Delhi, India (22.4 million)
Mumbai, India (22.3 million)
New York City, United States (21.9 million)
São Paulo, Brazil (21 million)
Manila, Philippines (19.2 million)
Los Angeles, United States (18 million)
Shanghai, China (17.9 million)
Osaka, Japan (16.7 million)
Calcutta, India (16 million)
Karachi, Pakistan (15.7 million)
Guangzhou, China (15.3 million)
Jakarta, Indonesia (15.1 million)
Cairo, Egypt (14.8 million)
Buenos Aires, Argentina (14.1 million)
Moscow, Russia (13.5 million)
Beijing, China (13.2 million)
Dhaka, Bangladesh (13.1 million)
Istanbul, Turkey (12.5 million)
Rio de Janeiro, Brazil (12.5 million)
Tehran, Iran (12.5 million)
London, United Kingdom (12.3 million)
Lagos, Nigeria (11.4 million)

Source: Thomas Brinkhoff: The Principal Agglomerations of the World, 2009

the Tokyo metropolitan area has a population roughly the same as that of Canada or California! Determining these rankings is extremely difficult. Even the experts can't always agree.

Can you think of reasons why it would be so difficult to define a city and to count its people with some accuracy? Why are so many people attracted to huge cities? What do they offer? What are some of the problems associated with giant metropolitan areas? Would *you* want to live in a megacity? Why?

Declining Rural Populations

As cities grow throughout much of the world, rural populations decline in many places. Particularly in the world's economically less developed countries, rural life can be extremely difficult. There, many people are self-sufficient; they live outside the cash economy. They produce, make, or otherwise provide everything that they need. Should exchanges take place, they are most often conducted by simple barter (trade). Opportunities for individual advancement are extremely limited, as are facilities and services. Schools, health care, sanitation, and entertainment are substandard, if they exist at all. In much of the world, a huge and ever-widening gap exists between rural "have nots" and urban "haves." Because of the differences in quality of life, urban centers will continue to grow in size. As this happens, rural populations will continue to decline.

The Lure of "Amenity" Locations

A half century ago, most people lived in cities, towns, or on productive farmland. That is where they could make a living. Few people lived in "amenity" locations. These are places that offer some particular feature that people find attractive. Coasts, lakeshores, and mountains are examples. Some people are attracted to warm climates. Others are drawn to a location by its historical or cultural attractions. Most such areas were once relatively inaccessible and poorly developed. They offered few jobs. There simply was nothing to attract people to such places.

Ninety-one percent of Australia's inhabitants live in urban areas such as Melbourne (above). Each country defines "urban area" differently. Australia considers an urban center to be a population cluster of 1,000 or more, with a density of 200 people per square kilometer.

As a result, most coasts, lakeshores, mountains, mining ghost towns, and other historic centers attracted very few people. Today, however, many such areas are booming. What changed to make them so attractive? Why have areas previously avoided suddenly become some of the most desirable—and costly—locations in the United States, Canada, and many other developed countries?

Answers to the foregoing questions can be found in social and cultural change. Today, many people have jobs that do not tie them to a particular place. Improved transportation and communication facilities have made remote living much easier and more pleasant. The computer has brought information to the fingertips of people almost anywhere. In most developed countries, industrial jobs have given way to service-oriented tasks, many of which are no longer tied to a particular place. Many retirees now have savings, pensions, or other sources of income that make them financially independent. And they, of course, can retire where they like. As population grows, amenities, services, and facilities also increase. Life becomes increasingly comfortable and enjoyable, the area attracts more people, and the cycle continues.

GLOBAL TRENDS

Many factors help to explain changes in population density and distribution. This is true both locally and globally. Many towns and cities grow, while others wither away. Rural areas throughout much of the world are experiencing population decline. On a global scale, several factors cause populations to change. Some areas grow in population because of high rates of natural increase. This is occurring in much of Africa and portions of southern and southwestern Asia. Elsewhere, as in much of Europe, zero population growth has been achieved. Nearly half of the continent's countries are experiencing a negative rate of natural increase. This means that more people die each year than are born.

A major shift is occurring in population density and distribution as a result of migration. Each year, tens of millions of people move from one country to another. This, of course, results in not only a change in population distribution, but in density as well. One area loses population (for instance, the Snow Belt or the Great Plains), while another gains population (the Sun Belt).

Changes in population distribution and density can have a good or bad impact. Throughout much of the world, millions of people are leaving the countryside. They are moving to cities in search of a better life. But this massive rural-to-urban migration has both positive and negative effects. As people leave the country, rural development often suffers. When an area has fewer people, there is less incentive for a country to spend limited resources developing transportation linkages. Schools, health care facilities, and other services may decline or vanish. Economic productivity suffers as people leave their fields or flocks. Rural underdevelopment is a serious problem in many places. This is particularly true in many LDCs.

Throughout much of the world, urban populations are exploding. This is particularly true in less developed lands. Unfortunately, many if not most of them are poorly equipped to meet the needs of booming populations. In poor countries, huge slums surround nearly every city. These squatter settlements may hold as much as half of the urban population. Yet, they often lack many essential facilities and services. Clean water or safe sewage and garbage disposal may be inadequate or lacking altogether. The same holds true for police protection, public transportation, schools, and other services. Jobs are scarce and unemployment is high.

As you learned in Chapter 2, populations change in response to four factors: births, deaths, in-migration, and out-migration. In the following chapter, you will see how migration affects populations and settlement. You will also learn about some of the ways in which migration can help, or sometimes hinder, a region's social and economic stability.

PEOPLE ON THE MOVE

Within your school or neighborhood, how many new faces have appeared within the past year? How many people moved away? Have you moved during your lifetime? People—particularly those living in the United States and Canada—seem to be on the move constantly. According to census data, the typical Northern American moves more than a dozen times during his or her lifetime. This chapter is about migration, the movement of people from place to place. It discusses reasons why people move and where they decide to go. Past, present, and probable future migration patterns will also be discussed. Finally, the chapter explains how migration plays a major role in affecting global connections.

THE HUMAN HABITAT

Among Earth's life forms, humans are unique in many ways. One unique trait is our ability to greatly expand the *human habitat*—

the environments in which we are able to survive. Humans live and thrive in many environments for which we are not physically (biologically) suited. Only humans have this ability. All other life forms are limited to a particular habitat to which they are physically adapted. For humans, on the other hand, *culture*—our knowledge, tools, and skills—is our adaptive mechanism.

Most scientists believe that humans began in and are biologically adapted to humid tropical climates. Yet today we occupy all of Earth's diverse environments. Several thousand even live in parched desert regions. Thousands more live in research stations on the frigid Greenland and Antarctic ice caps. How are we able to do this? Humans are the only animal capable of artificially creating heat. We can also create protective clothing and shelter, and produce and store food. These are just some of the things that make it possible for humans to occupy any and all of Earth's environments.

MOVING AND MIGRATING

Millions of people move, or change their place of residence, each year. They may move from one apartment to another in the same complex. Or they may move from one continent to another, traveling halfway around the world in the process. In either case, they are said to *move*, which is a catchall word for people on the go. If a person moves across a political boundary, he or she *migrates*, that is, becomes a *migrant*. *Internal migration* is from one political unit of a country, such as a state or province, to another. Someone moving from South Dakota to Arizona or from Ontario to Alberta would statistically be counted as an internal migrant. *International migration* involves moving from one country to another, as from the United States to Canada or from Mexico to the United States.

No one knows how many people change their place of residence each year. The number certainly must be very high, perhaps hundreds of millions. Better data are available for migration because migrants cross political boundaries. In so doing, they change the population in not one but two political units. According to the United Nations, an estimated 200 million people migrate each year. That is about 3 percent of the world's population. Approximately 60 percent of these migrants, or about 120 million of them, move from less developed countries (LDCs) to industrialized lands. They do so for many reasons, but most are searching for a better life.

Although this chapter's emphasis is on people who move, it is important to note that most people never do (at least very far). In fact, it is estimated that more than 75 percent of the human population is fairly stationary. That is, they never move more than a few miles, if at all, from their place of birth.

Many extreme environments that were previously uninhabitable have been adapted to be suitable for human life. For example, thanks to irrigation and cooling systems, people can live comfortably in desert conditions such as in the U.S. Southwest (above).

MIGRATION AND POPULATION CHANGE

Do you recall the demographic equation, the formula for determining population change? Births and deaths, of course, are a very important factor. But for many places in the world today, out-migration and in-migration are the most significant contributors to population change. Many rural areas, for example, are experiencing a sharp drop in population because of emigration (out-migration). Many cities, on the other hand, are bursting at their seams with population growth resulting from a flood of immigrants.

There are three key facts to remember in regard to migration. First, births (fertility) and deaths (mortality) have biological limits. Only the total population imposes a limit on potential migration. In theory, at least, everyone alive today could move. Second, a birth or a death changes the population of only one place. Migration changes the population of two locations. Finally, migration is selective and mainly voluntary. It occurs for various reasons and does not happen to everyone.

PUSH AND PULL FACTORS

Why do people move? And when they move, what factors influence where they go? Such decisions are often quite complex and can be swayed by many considerations. Moving is a two-part decision. First, a person must decide (or be forced) to leave a place of residence. Some factor or factors influenced the decision to move. Demographers call these forces *push factors*. They can be determined by the person or persons who move or can be imposed by conditions beyond one's control.

Once the decision is reached to move, one must decide where to go. In theory, at least, a person could move any place in the world. Imagine that you decide to move but do not yet have a destination. Think for a moment about those places in the world to which you would not want to go. What factors influenced your decisions? Now think about those places to which you would not mind moving. What conditions drew you to these particular locations? This exercise illustrates a very important reality. For countless reasons, much of the world is unattractive to most migrants. For some, language, religion, economic conditions, or political status pose a barrier. For others, physical features such as weather and climate or terrain are deterrents. Certain areas, however, are attractive. They offer conditions that lure migrants. These are *pull factors.*

MAKING CONNECTIONS

THE MIGRATION "BRAIN DRAIN"

It is widely known that, in many areas, businesses and industries are unable to find well-educated, highly trained American workers. They must turn to workers from Asia and elsewhere to fill positions. This problem is not limited to the United States. It is commonplace throughout much of the economically developed world.

When a country's own labor force is unable to meet its need for workers, the obvious solution is immigration. But when well-educated, highly skilled people leave their homeland, the result is a "brain drain." Most such migrants are from poor, less developed countries. When they leave, they take with them human talent that could contribute to that country's own development. Is this fair? As is true of so many issues, answers do not come easily. Money sent home by citizens working abroad is a leading source of income in many LDCs. In Mexico, for example, it is the second leading source of revenue! As developed countries continue to age, even more jobs—both low paying and highly skilled—will become vacant. Most of them will be filled by migrants. The brain drain, if anything, will become even greater. And both developed and less developed countries will benefit from this arrangement.

Throughout history, the primary pull factor has been economic gain. People changed locations in hope of improving their economic well-being, hence, their quality of life. Even today, most people move for economic reasons. Where they go is determined by the belief that their income, and therefore their life, will improve. Early humans were lured by the prospect of finding better hunting, fishing, and gathering grounds. Later, many agricultural people were attracted by available land or better soil. During recent centuries, urban populations have boomed as people flocked from poor rural environments to cities in search of jobs. Today, millions of people are moving from poor countries to economically developed regions in North America, Europe, and elsewhere.

On an individual basis, there are many reasons why people decide to emigrate (exit, or move out). The same holds true for those factors that influence immigration (moving in). In some places, life has become difficult because of human-caused conditions. War, political conflict, and discrimination (whether racial, social, religious, ethnic, or other) have long influenced emigration. Various physical conditions can also force people to emigrate. Natural disasters such as fire, flood, drought, earthquake, or volcanic eruption can make a place difficult if not impossible to live in. Communities can die because mines close as ore plays out.

WHO MOVES?

Certain groups of people are more apt to move than others. Young people, for example, tend to be much more mobile than established middle-aged individuals. The young are less apt to have strong ties to a particular place. They are also more adaptable and better able to accept major changes in their lives. And, of course, as they begin careers, they are more apt to seek or change employment. As young people marry, in most instances the union involves one or both parties changing their place of residence.

Elderly people may also move. In economically developed countries, older people often move after retirement. Many retirees in the United States and Canada, for example, are drawn to a Sun Belt location. There, they need not shovel snow, and outdoor recreational activities such as golf can be pursued throughout the year. Others are drawn to places that offer adequate health and medical services. In traditional societies, many elderly move in with one of their children.

Single people are much more apt to move than are married couples. Men, except in the case of marriage, are more apt to move than women. People who are unemployed or underemployed (they have jobs but receive very low pay) are quite mobile. They move in search of a job or higher paying employment. People who are well established in a job and happy with their employment are the least apt to move. An exception is well-educated professionals who possess skills that give them many options. Physicians, nurses, pharmacists, attorneys, accountants, and many others can be quite selective in where they want to live. They often move to places they find more attractive.

MOVEMENT OF EARLIEST HUMANS

Movements of early humans were largely local. Equatorial East Africa is believed to have been the homeland of humankind. *Homo sapiens* (humankind) is a tropical animal. We begin to feel the effects of cold when exposed to temperatures lower than 77°F (25°C). Many developments had to occur before we could leave the tropics and venture into the much cooler middle latitudes. Of greatest importance, perhaps, was control of fire. Protective clothing was needed, as was some kind of shelter. Techniques for working with stone had to be developed so that sharp tools and weapons could be made. Only when these and many other traits were available could early people begin to leave the tropics and move into more challenging climates.

Archaeologists (scientists who study early peoples) believe that humans spread throughout Africa at least one million years ago. Not long thereafter, they reached and spread across much of Europe and Asia. Conditions in the mid-latitudes were much colder than in the tropical African homeland. Through cultural adaptation, humans had made a huge step toward expanding the environments in which they could live.

Before they could spread across the remainder of Earth's surface, watercraft had to be developed. Open water proved to be a much greater barrier to early migration than were land conditions. In fact, throughout more than 95 percent of human history, settlement was limited to the Afro-Eurasian landmass. Evidence suggests that expanses of open sea water were first spanned only about 50,000 years ago. That is when humans first appeared in Australia. To reach the island continent at that time in geological history would have involved at least one water crossing of about 44 miles (71 km).

PEOPLING OF THE AMERICAS

Who were the first Americans? Where did they come from? How, when, and by what route did they arrive? These questions remain unanswered and continue to be hotly debated by scientists today. One theory holds that big game hunters crossed *Beringia*—the Bering Strait land bridge between Asia and North America. At the time, sea level was about 400 feet (122 m) lower than it is today. According to this theory, people simply crossed on the dry land that then joined the two continents. Sea level was lower because so much of Earth's water supply was locked up on land in the form of glacial ice.

After reaching North America, these early wanderers moved southward, passing through a 1,200-mile-long (2,000 km) ice-free corridor between two huge ice sheets. Around 13,000 years ago, they supposedly arrived in present-day New Mexico. This early culture takes its name from a city near which their unique projectile points were first found, Clovis.

Recent archaeological finds in both North and South America cast considerable doubt on the Beringia-Clovis theory. New data from a number of archaeological sites suggest that humans were in the Americas several thousand years before an ice-free corridor could have formed. A rapidly growing body of research suggests that the earliest Americans may have followed a coastal route. Some scientists even believe that they may have traveled by water, at least part of the way.

During the Ice Age, much of the land now submerged beneath the sea was exposed above the level of the sea. People simply could have walked on this land and perhaps rafted around barriers such as glaciers entering the sea. The coastal environment would have been much less challenging than an interior route. Weather would have been much milder. Fresh water would have been plentiful, as would plant and animal life for food, shelter, and clothing. Abundant driftwood could be used for fuel and other purposes, including the building of rafts.

EXPANDING THE ECUMENE

There are many ways of knowing that humans have long been on the move. The present-day distribution of various physical features, for example, provides clues. Such human conditions as stature, skin color, eye color and shape, blood type, and DNA prove widespread migration. People of Mongoloid physical stock are an excellent example of early movement. This racial group began in Central or East Asia. Today, however, they are indigenous (native) to all inhabited continents except Australia.

By the dawn of the common era, all of the world's ecumene (the roughly two-thirds of Earth's land surface that is occupied by humans) was settled. The very last frontier to be occupied was the vast Pacific Basin. Even there, most islands were discovered and occupied by Polynesians at least 1,500 years before Magellan's early-sixteenth-century voyage.

There were, of course, a huge number of early migrations, and it is often difficult to trace their origins, routes, and destinations. A language map can offer many clues about them. Many Native American languages, for example, can be traced to Asian origins. Upon reaching the Americas, many early migrating groups split up and headed in separate directions. Today, similarities in language offer evidence of their ancient cultural ties. More recently, English—the native tongue of England—provides ample evidence of early British migration. It is the dominant language in the United States, much of Canada, Australia and New Zealand, portions of South Africa, and other former British colonies.

TYPES OF MIGRATION

Groups of people move for various reasons. There are many types of migration. Some moves are temporary, whereas others are permanent. In most cases, people move by choice; in other instances, they are forced to migrate. In nearly all cases, unless forced, people move in the belief that their lives will be better in a new location.

Free Migration

Historically, free or individual migration has been most common. It occurs when a family or an individual decide to move. How many moves have members of your family made? Did they make the decision to leave and where to go? If so, it was a move based upon free choice. Sometimes, large numbers of people will move from one area to another. Although the decision is free and individual, a mass movement of people, called a *stream migration*, takes place.

The largest voluntary stream migration in history involved the emigration of Europeans. Over a span of several centuries, more than 60 million of them moved to the Americas, Australia and New Zealand, South Africa, and elsewhere. Their reasons for migrating varied, although nearly all of them sought a better life. Most were drawn by the prospect of economic gain, including the dream of land ownership. Others sought freedom to practice their religion without persecution. Many simply wanted to free themselves from the Old World's rigid socioeconomic system.

Forced Migration

Some migrations are forced. They are involuntary, or impelled. The slave era provides a tragic example of this type of human movement. Between the sixteenth and mid-nineteenth centuries, an estimated 6 to 9 million Africans were unwillingly transferred to the Americas as slaves. Of these, 6 percent, or between 360,000 and 540,000, were enslaved in the United States. Millions of others were forced into labor in Europe and Asia. Worldwide, there are millions of refugees who have been forcibly displaced from their homes.

Restrictions on Movement

A few countries place restrictions on emigration and/or immigration. People are not allowed to enter the country, move about freely within it, or leave. In a few countries, particularly communistic totalitarian states, emigration and immigration are largely prohibited. The former Soviet Union had such a policy. Today, North Korea and Cuba are among the few countries that continue to restrict the movement of citizens.

Nearly all countries have laws that limit immigration. Throughout much of its history, the United States has had among the world's most liberal immigration laws. In fact, the United States has welcomed more immigrants than all other countries combined! Today, however, the United States faces a difficult demographic, social, and political issue. More than 12 million undocumented immigrants are believed to be in the country. Most are from Latin America, and about half of them are from

Mexico. What political action, if any, should be taken in response to this situation is hotly debated.

MIGRATION TODAY

The number of international migrants has reached an all-time high. In 2005 (the last year for which data are available), there were 191 million migrants, or 3 percent of the world's population. These are people who crossed international boundaries and stayed outside their country of citizenship for at least one year. Much of today's migration is from economically less developed countries to developed countries. In the Middle East, for example, more than 80 percent of the residents of the small, but wealthy, United Arab

(continues on page 92)

Migration alters population data. This includes forced migration, such as when people are driven out of their land. Above, refugees from Zimbabwe seek asylum at the border of South Africa in September 2008.

REFUGEES

Throughout history, people have been forced to migrate. In some cases, the move was forced by other people. Racial intolerance, racial and ethnic strife, economic conditions, and warfare have caused countless millions of people to relocate. So, too, have natural conditions such as drought, loss of soil fertility, climate change (as during the Ice Age), and famine. People forced to move as a result of conditions beyond their control are called refugees (people who seek refuge in another land). According to the United Nations, a refugee is any person who:

> owing to a well-founded fear of being persecuted for reasons of race, religion, nationality, membership of a particular social group, or political opinion, is outside the country of their nationality, and is unable or, owing to such fear, is unwilling to avail himself of the protection of that country.

You may have noticed that the UN definition does not include people who are forced to relocate because of famine or environmental causes. It is limited to people who seek protection from oppression, or human-imposed cruelty. Refugees who seek to escape such conditions become asylum seekers in another location. In 2008, according to various estimates, there were between 10 and 21 million refugees worldwide. These are the people who were forced to leave their country of citizenship and seek asylum in another land. An estimated 20 million others have been internally displaced. These are people who have been forced to leave their homes and move elsewhere within their own country.

The actual number of refugees is impossible to determine. This is why figures vary greatly. Not all countries, for example, define "refugee" in the same way. Many governments will not admit that their citizens are oppressed and forced to move. Another major problem is simply finding refugees, many of whom are constantly on the move.

Finally, there are the issues of accurate census documentation and legal as opposed to illegal status.

In the United States alone, there are an estimated 12 million to as many as 20 million undocumented residents. Certainly some of these people would qualify for "refugee" status according to the United Nations definition. According to the UN High Commission for Refugees (UNHCR), more than 150 countries (out of a total of about 200) now have refugee populations. These are divided among refugees, asylum seekers, returned refugees, internally displaced people, and stateless persons. The largest refugee movement in history took place after the 1947 division of the Indian subcontinent into India and Pakistan. An estimated 30 million people, primarily Hindus and Muslims, fled their homelands to avoid religious persecution. Hindus moved from present-day Pakistan and Bangladesh to India. Most Muslims moved from India to Pakistan and Bangladesh.

According to the most recent UN data (January 2006), there are approximately 21 million refugees worldwide. Of these, 8.6 million, or 42 percent, are in Asia, and another 5.2 million, or 25 percent, are in Africa, where refugees have fled to more than 20 countries. Combined, these two troubled regions have produced about two-thirds of the world's total refugee population.

In 2008, the greatest numbers of documented refugees fled five countries. According to UN figures, war-torn Iraq leads with 2.2 million emigrants, followed closely by strife-ridden Afghanistan, from which 2 million people have fled. Three African countries—Sudan, Somalia, and the Democratic Republic of the Congo—follow closely behind in the number of emigrants with refugee status. These figures, however, tell only part of the story. In war-torn Sudan, for example, as many as 5 million people have been displaced internally. Here, centered in the Darfur region, a tragedy has unfolded that the United Nations calls "the world's worst humanitarian crisis."

(continued from page 89)

Emirates are immigrants. Between 1985 and 2005, the number of people moving from poor to industrialized countries more than doubled from 55 million to 120 million. Clearly, the dream of economic gain and a better life continues to be the primary underlying push factor and pull factor influencing migration.

FUTURE GLOBAL CONNECTIONS

Migration is difficult to predict. Fifty years ago, who could have foreseen the massive migration from the U.S. Snow Belt to the warm Sun Belt? Or, for that matter, that rural-to-urban migration would cause an unparalleled boom in urban populations throughout much of the less developed world? Who could have foreseen that many developed world cities would actually lose populations as people moved to the suburbs and beyond? Several trends do seem likely to occur during coming decades in regard to migration. All of them will result in increased global connections.

First, migration itself may increase. In Europe, for example, within the European Union (EU), most restrictions on international migration have been removed. Second, migration will result in a greater blending of races and cultures. At the local scale, this will result in much greater diversity. One benefit is that people will be offered many more cultural options such as food and music. Globally, however, it will have an opposite effect. Worldwide, things will become more alike, hence, "bland."

Third, a rapidly aging population in the developed world will create a huge age imbalance. This, in turn, will create a worker shortage that will accelerate migration streams from LDCs to industrial nations. Fourth, rural-to-urban migration will increase in LDCs, as a growing number of people move to cities in search of a better life. In some developed lands, including the United States, just the opposite will occur. People will continue to flee the crowded cities. As this occurs, smaller cities, suburbs, rural communities, and the countryside will grow in population. Fifth, population growth in the developed world will depend increasingly upon immigration, rather than natural increase. In the United States, immigration currently accounts for 70 percent of population growth. Finally, the world population continues to grow. This growth surely will result in expansion of the ecumene. Much of Earth's surface supports a very low population density. As the human population grows toward the 9 billion mark, many areas of low population density will begin to attract migrants.

CAN EARTH CONTINUE TO PROVIDE?

Two centuries ago, Thomas Malthus doubted that Earth could continue to provide for the rapidly growing population of his time. There was widespread fear that natural resources were running out. Food was scarce, hunger was widespread, and famine was commonplace. It seemed that people were everywhere. Sickness was common, and life expectancy was short. Malthus and many others believed that there simply was not enough food, space, or other life requirements for everyone. They were confident that an exploding human population was the root of the problem. If nothing was done to slow population growth, the results would be catastrophic. Clearly, something had to be done. At the time, the world population was perhaps 900 million, or about one-seventh of today's 6.7 billion.

Do you remember the "gloom-and-doom" book titles listed in Chapter 3? Most of them were published 50 to 60 years ago. The fears expressed by their authors were basically the same as those about which Malthus cautioned in the late 1700s. During the mid-1900s, scientists, environmentalists, and others who voiced population-related concerns gained a title. They were called *neo (new)-Malthusians*. Their message was similar to that expressed by Malthus; only the times (and population) had changed.

Since the mid-1960s, the population has more than doubled. As has been discussed previously, most data clearly support the belief that the human population has never been better off than it is today. People are eating better and have a much higher standard of living than ever before. They are living longer and healthier lives than at any previous time in history. It makes one wonder, "What's going on here?" This chapter attempts to explain the relationship between population and Earth's ability to provide for human needs.

EARTH'S LIMITS

Social scientists and others have long attempted to identify Earth's limits to provide for a growing human population. Does Earth actually have limits in terms of adequately providing for constantly growing numbers of people? Of course it does! It seems absurd to believe that Earth could support a population of, say, 100 billion people. The real question we must ask, then, is "At what point are Earth's limits reached?" And is, in fact, that limit based on numbers of people or the standard of living of the population? An increasing number of experts believe that how people live is more important than how many people are alive. The United States, after all, has about 5 percent of the world's people, but it consumes about 25 to 30 percent of all resources and raw materials.

Spaceship Earth

During the 1960s, several American writers popularized the idea of Earth as a spaceship. At the time, the Soviet Union and the United States were locked in a space race. By the end of the decade, American astronauts had reached the Moon. For the first time ever, Earth could be viewed from distant space. The planet appeared as a small "spaceship" in the vastness of the universe. Like a well-stocked space vehicle, Earth has resources. Yet like a space vehicle, our planet is a closed environment. Nothing of importance (other than solar energy) comes in or, for that matter, goes out. Humans are dependent upon Earth and its resources just as astronauts are dependent upon their space capsule and its contents. The similarity between Earth and a spaceship made a powerful analogy. Many people immediately began to adopt the

CARRYING CAPACITY

Carrying capacity is an idea that is widely used by demographers, geographers, environmentalists, the media, and others. Basically, it refers to the number of people a particular area and its conditions can support. The concept comes from rangeland management. A rancher, for example, needs to know how many head of cattle can be grazed on a particular plot of land. This number is determined by several factors, including the condition of the range or pasture. If too many head of livestock are placed in an area, they will overgraze the pasture. With vegetation cover gone, the animals may go hungry or even suffer and starve. Further, in the absence of grass cover, the soil may be swept away by erosion, thereby contributing to still worse destruction of the land and plant cover.

On the surface, both the spaceship Earth and carrying capacity ideas seem to make sense. Yet do these two factors really determine the planet's ability to provide for a growing population? If they do, how can one explain the steady improvement in human well-being, despite history's greatest spurt of population growth? Clearly, there are other important factors that must be considered. Cultural factors—what people actually do with the land and its resources—rather than the environment itself are the major determinants of a region's carrying capacity.

idea. They used it to question the planet's carrying capacity, its ability to support a growing population.

THE "ADAM AND EVE" DILEMMA

It has been said that Earth was overpopulated when it was home to only two people, "Adam and Eve"! How could that possibly be true? Imagine that you were one of the earliest humans to occupy our planet. What things in your surroundings were useful to you? In fact, what things could you have used? Could you have tilled the soil? Could you have made metals from the minerals locked away in the earth? Did you have tools to cut huge trees? What things within your surroundings were "natural resources"? (A natural resource is anything within the natural environment that is used by humans.)

To answer this question, we can look to other higher primates. They drink water, eat plants and/or other animals, and live "very close to nature." Certainly it was this way with early humans through perhaps the first half of human history. Their resource base was extremely limited. They did not know that many things, such as useful minerals, even existed. For many of the things of which they were aware, they had no way of putting them to use. What was their resource base in terms of area? How far could they travel to obtain things that they needed? (Remember, even today most humans never travel more than a few miles from their birthplace.) Were early people able to preserve perishable food and resources?

Through time, of course, people made the environment in which they lived much more productive. They gradually expanded their living area, making it possible to find and use resources from "over the hill." As their awareness and knowledge increased, early humans were able to use more things in their environment. Through time, better tools and weapons made more food available. Something as simple as using a hollowed-out gourd as a container was a huge step forward. It

In 2008, people in many countries around the world—including Egypt (*above*)—rioted to protest rising food prices. According to CNN, World Bank president Robert Zoellick said the surging costs could set back the fight against worldwide poverty by seven years.

became possible to both carry and store water and food. With each development, spaceship Earth became more productive and its carrying capacity grew by leaps and bounds. As more food and other resources became available, the human population began to grow.

In the previous paragraph, you were reminded once again of the importance of culture—what humans know and are able to do because we are human. Spaceship Earth offers solid material, water, air, and both plant and animal life. During particular periods of geologic history, these elements remain fairly constant. What has changed is the human ability to use them. As knowledge, tools, techniques, and other aspects of our culture have expanded, humans have vastly increased Earth's productivity. The author will use his surroundings of eastern South Dakota to illustrate the importance of culture in making the environment productive.

A LESSON FROM SOUTH DAKOTA

South Dakota's earliest residents hunted and gathered. Although some Native Americans eventually farmed, those on the Interior Plains were unable to do so. They did not have any means of breaking and turning the thick, fertile sod. Yet it was this sod that helped make the region's soil some of the world's most fertile. Hunting supported a very low population and population density. People lived in small, scattered bands with a density of perhaps one person per hundred square miles.

During the last half of the nineteenth century, eastern South Dakota was homesteaded. People settled on small plots of land called homesteads on which they could live and raise a family. Horses, mules, and oxen were the beasts of burden. With the introduction of a steel-tipped plow and draft animals, the thick sod could be broken. Yet fields were small, tilling was primitive, crops were poor, and yields were low. Today, the same plot of land can produce a crop yield perhaps 20 times greater than that of a century ago. As production grew, so did the rural population.

Over time, many agricultural developments greatly expanded crop production and yields. Tractors and other modern equipment made it possible to farm much greater areas. Instead of several acres of land tilled for crops, today's average South Dakota farm occupies an area of about 2.5 square miles (6.5 sq km). The carrying capacity of land has vastly increased. Today, a single farmer can produce enough food to feed hundreds, or even thousands, of people depending upon what is grown.

Sioux Falls is South Dakota's largest city, with about 200,000 people in the metropolitan area. The average family income in the city is approaching $60,000. With an average family size of 2.38 people, that amounts to more than $5 billion in family income each year. Sioux Falls spreads out over an area of about 70 square miles (150 sq km), the area covered by 28 average-sized South Dakota farms. Income generated by the city is hundreds of times greater than that which the same area would produce if farmed. When converted to urban land use and economic development, the land's carrying capacity soared. Yet the natural environment, itself, has not changed. What has changed is the way the land and other resources are used. The result has been that a once rather sleepy town has become one of the nation's fastest growing metropolitan areas both in population and income.

FOOD FOR THE FUTURE

As the world's population continues to expand toward 9 billion, the shadow of Thomas Malthus once again falls across the planet. Many people now wonder whether Earth can keep up with the food demands of a growing population. There seems to be ample fuel to feed their flames of fear. During 2007 and 2008, food riots occurred in many countries. The price of many foods, including in the United States and Canada, continues to climb rapidly. Rice, the world's major food staple, doubled in cost from 2007 to 2008. According to United Nations (UN) figures, an estimated 800 million people suffer from constant hunger worldwide. Five million young people starve to death each year. Many millions more lack the energy to work, play, or study hard. For even a single person to go to bed hungry is, of course, both tragic and inexcusable in a world of plenty. What is the situation? Can Earth actually provide enough food for everyone? Or has the limit foreseen by Malthus finally been reached?

Why Are So Many People Hungry?

Geographer William A. Dando wrote an eye-opening book entitled *The Geography of Famine*. It documents every famine throughout human history for which records exist. Hunger has been a constant companion of humans since the very beginning. Yet Dando's research clearly shows that the most devastating famines were long ago. The closer we come to the present day, the fewer their number and the less deadly they become. Fewer famines have occurred during the past half century—during which the human population has doubled—than during any other period in history.

Since Malthus's time, when food was scarce, nearly everyone pointed to a single "cause"—too many people. Overpopulation, they reasoned, was the problem. As their argument went, there simply was not enough food to go around. Actually, nothing could be farther from the truth. Until people recognize the source of the problem, it will continue to plague humankind. People will continue to suffer and die unnecessarily. You already have seen that fewer people are hungry today, as a percentage of the human population, than at any time in history. So, you are probably asking, "What *is* the problem?"

In 2000, the magazine *U.S. News & World Report* carried an article based upon a UN study that identified the world's top-ten countries with "Empty Stomachs." The article pointed to overpopulation as the source of the problem. Countries included in the list, and the percentage of their population that was underfed in 2000, are as follows:

Somalia	75%
Afghanistan	70%
Burundi	60%
Eritrea	65%
Haiti	62%
Congo (DRC)	61%
Mozambique	58%
North Korea	57%
Ethiopia	49%
Liberia/Niger	46%

Do you see a pattern? Can you think of things that many of these countries share in common *other* than hunger? During the late 1990s, for example, most of them were locked in bloody conflicts. Much of their rural population had fled to cities, or even left the country, to seek a safe haven elsewhere. Not one of the countries had a stable government at the time. Several of them were under the control of warlords and, for all practical purposes, were without any political leadership whatsoever. When government fails, so does a country's economy. When people are forced from their farms, a country's agricultural system will

MAKING CONNECTIONS

CHINA'S RISING STANDARD OF LIVING

The author teaches a course in Geography of the Future. More than a decade ago, he told students that China's rapidly expanding economy and standard of living posed a huge challenge to humankind. Needless to say, many students were quite upset about the idea. How, after all, could a better life for 20 percent of the world's people be a problem? Today, however, this view is being shared by many others. China has a population of 1.3 billion—more than four times as many people as live in the United States. As its economy booms, so does the country's demand for food, fuel and other resources, and raw materials. In fact, some observers point to China's growing demands as a primary cause of high gas prices, the rise in food prices, and many other global problems.

When incomes rise, diets improve. People want more and better food. In particular, they increase their consumption of meat (unless they are vegetarian). During recent decades, China's economy has boomed. Most Chinese people are richer and better off than ever before. With more money to spend, their diet has improved greatly.

collapse. In a domino effect, as the farm economy plummets, it drags the rest of the country's economy down with it. Now, people are unable to produce the food they need. With their country's economy weakened, they are too poor to buy food on the world market.

Can the World Be Fed?

Obviously, if one of every seven people in the world is hungry, something is wrong! But what? The answer is much more complex than many people realize. As you now know, the answer

Nowhere is this more evident than in the amount of meat that they are now eating. Livestock, however, are fed grain to be fattened for market. Many experts believe that China's economy will continue to grow at its recent rapid pace. If this happens, diets will continue to improve, resulting in the need for more grain to be imported. Some estimates suggest that, by 2025, the country will be buying as much grain as is currently sold in today's global market! This surely would cause the price of grain to skyrocket. Who would benefit from higher grain prices? Who would suffer as a result?

Can you think of problems that might result from a worldwide rise in the standard of living? For example, what would happen to the demand for fuel and other forms of energy? What about environmental pollution? Would people want more material possessions? In terms of buying, what would increase in addition to food consumption? These are serious questions that people need to begin asking. The future well-being of humankind depends upon their finding answers! Can you think of ways that living standards can continue to rise without causing huge problems for billions of people?

has little to do with the usual simplistic answer: "There are too many people." Numerous factors are involved, but here our attention will focus upon three of them that are closely related: production, marketing and distribution, and consumption.

Food Production

"There is not enough food to go around" is a nonissue in regard to the problem of feeding the world's population. Unfortunately, it is the one to which most people point when seeking an answer. Millions of people will needlessly continue to go to bed hungry each night until the real causes of hunger are recognized and acted upon. Let's take a close look at some of the facts about food production.

- Half of the world's potential agricultural land lies idle. Each year, the area of nonproducing land increases as people leave their rural homes for city life. As this happens, however, food production increases at a rapid pace because of better crops and farming methods.
- Half of the world's people are rice eaters, most of whom live in southern, southeastern, and eastern Asia. They are able to feed themselves with crops grown on land occupying an area about the size of North Dakota, South Dakota, and Nebraska.
- So productive are farmers in the United States that only about one percent of the population is engaged in agriculture. In fact, there are more people in prison or on parole than there are growing the nation's food!
- In many countries, including the United States, Canada, and Brazil, a growing amount of land is used to raise crops for fuel rather than food. Corn (maize), soybeans, and sugarcane are among the crops from which ethanol is produced. Rather than going into stomachs, potential food is going into gas tanks! Some people believe that this practice is responsible for the huge recent rise in

food prices. Yet in 2007, the U.S. Congress passed legislation that requires a fivefold increase in biofuel (fuel made from plants) production by 2022. Many experts believe that the rise of food prices has very little to do with raising crops for fuel.

- Looking ahead, some scientists believe that Earth's climate is warming. Should this actually happen, the growing season will lengthen. This will particularly benefit grain-growing regions of the United States, Canada, and interior Asia. These "breadbaskets" will be able to greatly expand their cropland and yields.
- Agricultural production throughout much of the world, particularly in the LDCs, is very low. Many things can and must be done to help increase productivity. The role of government, for example, was discussed previously. If farmers can make a profit, they will become more productive. Governments must ensure that rural people will be rewarded for their efforts. In many LDCs, it is all but impossible to make a living by farming, even at the subsistence level.

Earth's ability to produce biomass—plants and animals that can enter the food supply—is nearly unlimited. Certainly, enough food can be produced to feed the existing and projected future populations. A half century ago, agricultural production was given a huge boost by what came to be called the Green Revolution. Basically, it involved better strains of crop plants and farming techniques. Plants such as rice, maize, and wheat were improved to give higher yields. Irrigation, fertilizer, insect- and weed-killing chemicals, and other improvements also increased crop production.

Many scientists believe that agriculture is on the brink of an even greater breakthrough than the one brought on by the Green Revolution. They believe that genetic modification (GM)—changing a plant's genetic structure—can greatly increase crop yields. Not everyone agrees. Some people are deeply concerned about the idea of tinkering with genetics. There are concerns, for example, about human and environmental safety and other issues. A few critics go so far as to call GM crops "Frankenfoods" (after the Frankenstein character)! Of greatest importance is the fact that the technology is in place to make crops much more productive. We know that food production and quality (such as nutrients) can be increased greatly. Only time will tell whether GM crops will be widely accepted and their potential to help humankind realized.

Marketing and Distribution

If enough food is being produced to adequately feed the world's people, why are an estimated 800 million people still hungry? The answer to this question is both very simple and incredibly complex. Unfortunately, crop production is not evenly distributed across Earth's surface. Some places, such as parts of the United States and Canada, portions of China, and areas of Argentina and Brazil, produce huge yields. The United States, alone, is responsible for nearly one-half of all the world's food exports. Basically, the problem is: How can food be distributed from where it is produced to where it is needed?

Physically, massive amounts of food can be moved. Trucks, trains, barges, ships, and even huge cargo planes make shipping a nonissue to nearly all parts of the world.

The problem is economic: Who pays the grower? Who pays for distribution? Most of the world's hungry people live in poor, less developed countries. They simply cannot afford to buy food at market prices. In the United States and Canada, about 10 percent of the average family income is spent on food. In many poor countries, the figure rises to more thatn 50 percent and in some places even higher.

During the past decade, the gross national product of nearly all the world's countries has increased. In some lands, the gain

Food distribution—not simply the availability of food—is key to reducing hunger and poverty. Above, food is stored in the UN World Food Program warehouse in Kenya, awaiting distribution to Kenya, Sudan, Somalia, and Uganda.

has been substantial. Hopefully, this trend will continue. When people are able to purchase food, markets will increase and growers will respond. Nothing influences agricultural production like the opportunity to make a profit!

Consumption

What people eat also makes a difference. Kelp, a form of seaweed, is very nutritious. There is enough kelp in the Pacific Ocean, within a 100-mile (162 km) or so radius of nearly any coastal city, to feed the entire world population. It could be processed in many ways to vary taste, nutrients, and texture. But would *you* want to eat kelp three times a day, 365 days a year?

Diet is very difficult to change. It is one of the most deeply entrenched cultural practices. Consider, for example, the situation in India. It is a country with about 1.1 billion people, most of whom are Hindu. Hindus are vegetarians; they do not eat meat. Yet the country has an estimated 280 million cattle, more than twice as many as the United States. Because of religious beliefs, a huge potential food supply remains largely unused. But would you eat meat if you believed in reincarnation (rebirth in a new body)? After all, the flesh you ate might be that of a reborn relative!

More than half of the grain raised in the United States is used to feed livestock and poultry. This is an incredibly wasteful conversion. It can take up to 22,000 calories of grain and other forms of energy (such as fuel in transport) to put 400 calories of food on one's plate. Although wasteful and costly, it is a process that Americans, Canadians, and other wealthy societies can afford. Nonetheless, if people became vegetarians—stopped eating meat—the world's food supply could be increased greatly.

GLOBAL CONNECTIONS

The current population is approaching 7 billion, but the population is tightly clustered in a few areas. These areas are not necessarily those in which large amounts of food are produced. Globally, it is essential that ways be found to get food from places of production to those of need. This will not be an easy task. It will require the cooperation of people, agencies, and governments around the world. Yet as the population continues to grow, it becomes increasingly important that the food problem is solved.

The past half century has witnessed remarkable progress in feeding the world's people. Gains in food production, distribution, availability, and consumption have been huge. Yet in some areas of the world, people remain hungry. Erasing hunger is a challenge that will require global cooperation and even closer global connections.

8 LOOKING AHEAD TO 9.5 BILLION

What will the world be like midway into the twenty-first century when, according to United Nations estimates, the population will peak at between 9.0 and 9.5 billion people? That is a nearly 50 percent increase of today's population. Will Thomas Malthus's prediction finally come true? Will Earth's supply of food, water and other natural resources including fuel, and living space finally be pushed to the breaking point? Will humankind's fate, as Malthus warned, be a catastrophic drop in numbers? Will disease, famine, or war do what humans, themselves, seem incapable of doing—put a stop to population growth? This is the scenario that many alarmists foresee happening.

Some others, however, believe that there is less cause for alarm. In fact, they believe that the global condition is improving. People, they reason, are our most important "resource." They point to the fact that, throughout history, people have been able to solve problems, adapt to new resources, and otherwise improve living conditions. There is no reason to believe that knowledge, technology, and skills will not continue to improve. People are healthier and live longer lives today than during any previous time in human history. During recent decades, the standard of living and per capita incomes have greatly improved. So has literacy. Today, a greater percentage of people have at least some formal education than ever before. Education is the key factor that determines a person's future success.

What does the future hold in regard to adequate living space for a growing population? Will we run out of room to live? The answer to these questions is very clear: absolutely not! In fact, throughout much of the world, rural populations are in sharp decline as millions of people flee the countryside. When this happens, rural economies suffer; fields no longer produce, herds dwindle away, and villages wither. Particularly young adults flock to cities that offer jobs, education and health care, and many other attractions. The population and space issue was discussed at length in Chapter 5. Cities will continue to grow and many will become increasingly crowded. When traveling a large city freeway at rush hour, it is difficult to believe that Earth is not overcrowded. Yet remember, if each person on Earth occupied three square feet (1 sq m), the entire population would cover an area about the same size as a major U.S. or Canadian city.

What about natural resources? Alarmists have cautioned for decades that the planet is on the brink of running out of resources. A newspaper article that appeared in 1939 is a good reminder of "perspective." The article claimed that Earth's petroleum supply would be gone within 17 years, or by the mid-1950s. In the late 1950s, it was believed by some experts that many metals (iron, lead, zinc, copper, gold, and so forth) would be used up within several decades. Once gone, each of the ores would have to be replaced by something else. These experts predicted that the cost of the replacement material would be beyond the reach of most humans, causing a catastrophic drop in the global economy and standard of living by the 1970s. That did not happen.

It is obvious that certain limits do exist. Nonrenewable resources, those that cannot be replaced, may decline in importance and use, or even disappear. This has happened in the past and certainly will do so in the future. The price of some commodities, such as gold and petroleum, has skyrocketed during recent years. In 1970, gold was worth $35 an ounce; in late 2008, it was more than $800 an ounce. In January 1999, oil cost $8 a barrel. By June 2008, it was approaching $150 (only to drop to around $50 by November). What happened? Are we running out?

The value, and therefore the cost, of commodities is extremely complex. A great number of factors are involved. Despite what you may hear or read, there is plenty of gold and plenty of oil. Why, then, the meteoric increase in cost of these and other necessities? Once again, we must turn to culture, and particularly a society's values, for an answer.

Have you ever heard the expression "NIMBY" (Not In My Back Yard)? Nearly 30 years ago, South Dakota's Black Hills were one of the world's leading gold producers. There were a number of very productive mines. All of them have now been closed for a decade or more. Why? Did the gold play out? No. People became deeply concerned about the mines' impact on the environment. The mines and tailings (waste) dumps were an eyesore. The process of extracting gold, using poisonous cyanide to leach the ore, posed a serious threat to streams and groundwater. So much pressure was exerted on the mines that they simply closed.

Environmental concerns have also played a major role in skyrocketing oil prices. Who wants an oil refinery as a neighbor? This is one reason that (as of 2008) none have been built in the United States in more than three decades. Meanwhile, consumption of gasoline has more than doubled. As supplies become tighter, the price of gas creeps upward. Yet, U.S. coastal waters (the continental shelf) are believed to contain huge untapped reserves of oil. But they remain off-limits to drillers because of environmental concerns. The same holds true for

It is important that effective new methods be developed to ensure that Earth's resources are not depleted. Wind power and solar panels are two examples of alternative energy sources whose use is on the rise.

the development of Alaska's huge offshore oil and natural gas reserves. To tap these reserves, portions of the Arctic National Wildlife Refuge (ANWR) would be disturbed. Many people place the quality of a distant environment ahead of increasing the nation's oil supply.

A similar situation exists in much of the interior West of both the United States and Canada. Vast areas in both countries have rich deposits of oil shale (or tar sands) from which billions of barrels of oil could be extracted. Yet squeezing the oil out would involve strip mining, a process that would permanently scar the landscape. So far, development of this resource has been quite limited.

In summary, some resources eventually will become depleted. Others will become increasingly expensive, perhaps beyond the financial reach of many people. When faced with shortages, people always seem to find some substitute. Much of this "progress" is driven by the desire to make a profit. In the United States alone, for example, billions of dollars have been spent during the past decade in developing alternative energy sources.

During the coming decades, population growth will demand even closer global connections than those that exist today. Countries experiencing a sharp drop in their rate of population growth will depend increasingly upon immigrant labor. This will benefit the host lands. It will also be a tremendous financial boost to millions, perhaps hundreds of millions, of people from less developed countries. As this occurs, culture, too, will change. There will be much more blending of people and cultural traits and practices. Think about dining, for example. How many different ethnic foods (Mexican, Chinese, Italian, and so forth) can you select to eat within your area?

This book has stressed the fact that producing enough food to feed a growing world population is not a problem. Food distribution, perhaps, offers the greatest challenge to global connections. The economy of most less developed countries is growing, but slowly. How will these regions of the world be able to buy food and other resources? What impact will the rapidly rising economy of China and India have on world food and resource consumption, and therefore cost? These are just some of the questions and issues that humankind will face. Is your generation up to the challenge?

GLOSSARY

cohort A group of people who share a common time experience, such as baby boomers born following World War II (1946–1964).

crude birth/death rate Number of births/deaths per 1,000 people in a given population during a one-year period.

demography Scientific study of the human population with emphasis on statistical data, composition, change, and distributions.

dependency ratio The ratio of people in the dependent ages, usually those under 18 and those 65 or over, to those in their economically active years (18–64).

emigrant A person who emigrates, or leaves his or her country of residence to live elsewhere.

emigration Leaving one country or other political unit and taking up residence in another.

GDP–PPP Gross Domestic Product–Purchasing Power Parity A nation's GDP at PPP exchange rates is the value of that country's goods and services valued at U.S. prices.

Human Development Index (HDI) A United Nations ranking of countries from #1 to #177 in terms of human well-being based upon such factors as life expectancy, education, literacy, and standard of living.

immigrant An individual who moves from another country or political unit and takes up residence in a new land.

immigration The act of moving into a new country or other political unit to assume residence.

migration The physical act of moving from one political territory to another.

move To leave one place of residence for another, regardless of location.

rate of natural increase (RNI) Annual change in population resulting from growth or decline based upon births and deaths (expressed as a percent figure), the current world average being 1.1 percent to 1.2 percent.

rate of population change Increase or decrease in population resulting from births, deaths, emigration, and immigration (expressed as a percent figure).

zero population growth (ZPG) A condition in which a population remains steady, neither growing nor declining.

 BIBLIOGRAPHY 

Borgstrom, Georg. *The Food & People Dilemma.* North Scituate, MA: Duxbury Press, 1973.

Bugliarello, George. "Megacities and the Developing World." *The Bridge*, Vol. 29, No. 4 (Winter 1999). National Academy of Engineering.

Central Intelligence Agency. "The World Factbook." Available online. https://www.cia.gov/library/publications/the-world-factbook/

Dando, William A. *The Geography of Famine.* New York: John Wiley & Sons/Halsted Press, 1980.

Ehrlich, Paul R., and Anne H. Ehrlich. *Population, Resources, Environment: Issues in Human Ecology.* San Francisco: W.H. Freeman and Company, 1970.

Lappé, Frances Moore. *World Hunger: Twelve Myths.* New York: Grove Press, Inc., 1986.

Peters, Gary L., and Robert P. Larkin. *Population Geography: Problems, Concepts, and Prospects* (9/e). Dubuque, Iowa: Kendall/ Hunt Publishers, 2008.

Population Reference Bureau. *2008 World Population Data Sheet.* Washington, DC: Population Reference Bureau, 2008. http://www.prb.org/Publications/Datasheets/2008/2008wpds.aspx.

United States Census Bureau. Available online. http://www.census.gov.

FURTHER RESOURCES

Aaseng, Natham. *Over-Population: Crisis or Challenge?* New York: Franklin Watts, 1991.

Gritzner, Charles F. *Feeding a Hungry World*. New York: Chelsea House Publishers, 2009.

Hohm, Charles F., and Lori Justine Jones. *Population*. San Diego: Greenhaven Press, 2000.

Newton, David E. *Population: Too Many People*. Hillside, N.J.: Enslow Publishers, 1992.

Steele, Philip. *Population Growth*. Mankato, Minn.: Smart Apple Media, 2004.

Stewart. Gail. *Population*. Yankton, S. Dak.: Erickson Press, 2008.

WEB SITES

http://tigger.uic.edu/~rjensen/populate.html

World Population: A Guide to the WWW. Extremely useful Web site prepared by Richard Jensen (May 2007) with links to a vast array of population-related sites.

PICTURE CREDITS

Page

11: Rajanish Kakade / AP Images

15: Tsvangirayi Mukwazhi / AP Images

20: © Reuters/George Esiri/Landov

26: Courtesy of the U.S. Census Bureau

32: Shakeel Adil / AP Images

38: Schalk Van Zuydam / AP Images

43: © Infobase Publishing

45: Rajesh Kumar Singh / AP Images

47: © Infobase Publishing

52: Kamran Jebreili / AP Images

57: © Infobase Publishing

60: © Infobase Publishing

61: © Infobase Publishing

65: Courtesy of NASA/ Goddard Space Flight Center Scientific Visualization Studio; http://visibleearth.nasa.gov/view_rec.php?id=11793

75: www.shutterstock.com

80: Mike Fiala / AP Images

89: Denis Farrell / AP Images

98: Nasser Nasser / AP Images

107: Tom Maliti / AP Images

113: Mel Evans / AP Images

 INDEX 

INDEX

ABOUT THE AUTHOR

CHARLES F. "FRITZ" GRITZNER is Distinguished Professor of Geography at South Dakota State University in Brookings. He began college teaching and conducting geographic research in 1960. In addition to teaching, he enjoys travel, writing, working with teachers, and sharing his love for geography with readers. As a senior consulting editor and frequent author for Chelsea House Publishers' MODERN WORLD NATIONS, MAJOR WORLD CULTURES, EXTREME ENVIRONMENTS, and GLOBAL CONNECTIONS series, he has a wonderful opportunity to combine each of these "hobbies." Dr. Gritzner has served as both president and executive director of the National Council for Geographic Education and has received the council's highest honor, the George J. Miller Award for Distinguished Service to Geographic Education, as well as other honors from the NCGE, Association of American Geographers, and other organizations. He has taught population geography for nearly 50 years.